JOHN WILLIAMS V.C.

A Biography

JOHN WILLIAMS V.C.

A Biography

by

W. G. Lloyd

Best Wishes
W.G. Lloyd

Printed by

D. BROWN & SONS LTD
NORTH ROAD
BRIDGEND INDUSTRIAL ESTATE
BRIDGEND
CF31 3TP

© W.G. Lloyd, 1993

All rights reserved. No part of this publication may be reproduced, stored in a retrieval system, or transmitted, in any form or by means, electronic, mechanical, photocopying, recording or otherwise, without prior permission in writing from the publisher.

ISBN 0 9520543 2 9 (Hardback)

Published by W. G. Lloyd, Cwmbran, Gwent and printed by
D. Brown & Sons Ltd., North Road, Bridgend Industrial Estate, Bridgend, CF31 3TP

CONTENTS

Introduction

Chapter One	Early Life	9
Chapter Two	The Kaffir War	13
Chapter Three	The Zulu War	18
Chapter Four	Rorke's Drift	29
Chapter Five	For Valour	45
Chapter Six	The Valley of the Crow	52
Chapter Seven	Last Post	83
Chapter Eight	Epilogue	99
References		105
Appendix		107

INTRODUCTION

To enable me to write this biography I was fortunate to have lived in the town of Cwmbran for the past thirty years and within a few hundred metres of the perimeter of the Gwent Records Office. Although being born a few miles outside the town's northern border, my mother was of pure Cwmbran origin and how well I remembered her remarks about the upright gentleman of military bearing who fought the Zulus. My main regret is that I was not aware, at this very young age, of the importance of recording the events in the life of a great man and subsequently much information appears to have been lost forever with the passage of time.

When the decision was made to write the life story of the man behind the most treasured of all British medals, I embarked on the task of reading as much background material on the Anglo-Zulu War as possible. Very soon I became aware of the great amount of published material on the subject, that seemed to repeat itself time and time again. Upon the discovery of some small although important piece of information relating to the conflict, yet another book would appear on the market which contained the new but limited information dressed up in facts published many times before. Aware of this, I abandoned my task for a while until a great deal of parallel research revealed so much information about the life of John Williams in Cwmbran, that it became important for the later generations of the now large town, to be informed of what had gone before them.

The contents of this work are intended mainly for the folk of Cwmbran and the Eastern Valley of Gwent. If it is of interest to anyone further afield, I will be very pleased, and I wish to reiterate that the contents are not planned in any way to be an authoritive view of the Zulu conflict.

Some parts of the chapters relating to the war in South Africa are made up of the letters of the young men of the Eastern Valley of Monmouthshire (Gwent). They were on the spot, and who better could be found to convey that particular part of history than the young men who did the fighting. When reading these letters, it would be wise to understand that many of the young men had little formal education; the Board Schools had only just started by the time they were leaving school. Even so, their letters show a warmth and concern which is infrequently found in the few letters written by today's young men.

At this point I feel I should warn the reader that unusual circumstances arise which lead to the subject of this biography sometimes being referred to as John

Williams, and at other times John Fielding. The reason for this will become more apparent as the story unfolds, but I feel the confusion over this dual identity has meant this great story has gradually become lost to local people. This problem became more acute at the time of the construction of the large modern town of Cwmbran, when an influx of new residents arrived from many parts of the British Isles.

I wish to acknowledge the positive assistance of the following people who helped to make this book a privilege to research and collate:

Arthur and Aileen Johnston, Trevor and Nancy Daniels, Janet Gleeson, Joseph Fielding, John and Gillian Austin, Jan Wheeler and Jean Godfrey, of John Fielding House, Father J. Dominic Blaney, David F. Wait, Neil Evans, Ian Burlow, British Pathe News, The Press, The South Wales Argus, the Western Mail, the staff of the Newport Reference Library, Mr. A. Hopkins and his colleagues in the Gwent Records Office, the National Army Museum, the Imperial War Museum, Major R.P. Smith and his colleagues at the South Wales Borderers and Monmouthshire Regimental Museum of The Royal Regiment of Wales, and the senior residents of Cwmbran, whose comments were of tremendous value to the project.

W.G. Lloyd, 1993.

Chapter One

EARLY YEARS

Throughout the years, famine had periodically occurred in Ireland, but the great hunger of 1845-51 was unparalleled. To the poor of Ireland there was no such thing as money, the potato was the basic factor by which the value of labour was assessed. Landlords and farmers gave their labourers a cabin and a piece of potato ground, and rent in each case was worked off in days of labour for the landowner. The potato had become the vital part of the diet for those many thousands of poor people. The few lucky ones may have had a pig to sell for a few shillings, and this provided such clothing as the family possessed. With the fine quality produce being promptly exported, usually to England, the fear of famine was in the Irish people's blood, and the failure of the potato crop in 1845, soon produced the feeling that something very terrible was about to take place.

The crop failed again in 1846, and with only rotting potatoes to be seen in their allocated pieces of land, things were becoming desperate for the labouring class. Without any money to pay their rent, or, in many cases, too weak to work off the increasing debt, they were turned out of their cottages and forced to make hovels in some convenient ditch. Bands of starving men roamed the country begging for food. What there was of a Poor Law system in the country soon disintegrated and for the period up to 1851 it is estimated that 800,000 deaths from starvation and associated diseases occurred.

Thoughts turned to emigration. Some who could somehow raise the money, bought a passage to America or Canada. A few paid the large fee which would get them to Australia. Whichever destination in some far off country, Liverpool was to be the start of the long journey. Many decided on the short trip over the water, and chose to settle in either Scotland, England or Wales. These were the very poor, who only had to pay a few shillings for the passage, and in some cases their passage was free when they were used as ballast by the coal ships returning to Cardiff from Ireland. When arriving in Britain, they knew that under the English Poor Law system, no one would be allowed to die from starvation. In South Wales three towns were to feel the impact of this sudden invasion: Swansea, Cardiff and Newport, Monmouthshire. Very often the immigrants would not be welcome, and arrangements were made to drop off these destitute people on bleak parts of the Welsh coast. When ashore, they would move quickly and as far as possible inland, thus reducing the prospect of being immediately returned to Ireland.

Two young brothers, Michael and Maurice Fielding, were born in Ireland and experienced all the pain and suffering of the Irish people during this black period in Irish history. They were to follow the path of many who went before them, and left their beloved Ireland, never to return. Arriving in the border county of Monmouthshire in the early eighteen fifties, both hoped for a better life.

Their chosen area to settle had become Monmouthshire at the time of the 1543 Act of Union, and was, by its very culture and language, Welsh through and through. By placing the new county under the courts of Westminster, it became a county not wanted by the Welsh on one side, and not wanted by the English on the other side. So, the origins of many great and proud Monmouthshire men were decided.

With much of the noble county already ravaged by the greed of the iron and coal masters, the first sighting of Abergavenny, in the north, by the young Irishmen, must have caused them to wonder at this beautiful creation of God. The prospect of agricultural work would have immediately appeared highly promising. The ancient market town was delightfully situated at the confluence of the brook Gavenny with the river Usk - the latter being crossed by a charming ancient bridge of fifteen arches. It stands in the centre of four noted mountains. The Big Skirrid lies nearly to the north-east, the Little Skirrid more to the east, the Blorenge to the south-west, and the Sugar Loaf to the north-west.(1). Abergavenny was not unknown to the Irish people. Some ten years earlier, a small community of Irish folk existed in the town, with one street actually known as Ireland Street.

By 1855, Michael, aged 24 years, the elder of the two brothers, was working as an agricultural labourer in the nearby parish of Llanthewy Rhytherch, a scattered community of around ninety houses. He had by this time met and courted a nineteen year old spinster of Irish descent, by the name of Margaret Godsil. Michael married the Abergavenny girl, who, incidentally, was the daughter of a schoolmaster. The marriage took place on January 21st, 1855. After the service in the St. Michael's Catholic Chapel, his brother Maurice made his mark as a witness to the ceremony. The marriage certificate was to show that their father, Dennis Fielding, had by this time passed away, probably in Ireland. In August of the following year, Maurice, the younger brother, married Margaret Gill, another young lady who had been born in Ireland and who was at the time of the marriage, the daughter of Thomas Gill, master tailor, of Abergavenny.

Without the issue of the marriage of Michael and Margaret Fielding, this story could not be told. Thomas was their first born, and he was followed by John on May 24th, 1857, born at Merthyr Road, Abergavenny. John's baptism took place on the 26th May, 1857, in the old Franciscan mission which was the original parish church of Our Lady and St. Michael, Abergavenny. A new Catholic Church was built by 1860 and the old mission building, in recent years, became Dover's printing works. Father James Millward, Missionary Apostolic, who may have been of either the Franciscan Order, or the Order of St. Benedict, served at the early church from 1839 to 1857, and carried out the baptism ceremony. The entry in the baptism register gives Gulielmus Hart and Rosa Hansby as the godparents. Both young parents struggled to earn a living while staying in their rented accommodation in Merthyr Road, the part of the town which had by this time become a small Roman Catholic community. Little did they know that their second son would one day, with the use of an alias, become famous all over the world.

When John Fielding was around the age of five years, his father, in search of work as a labourer, moved the young family to the Cwmbran area and settled at number 3, Penywain Cottages, near St Dials, in the parish of Llantarnam.

Llanvihangel Llantarnam, better known by the latter name only, was a parish, found about four miles from Newport, and in the hundred of Usk (lower division). It was also present in the Newport union and county court district, the diocese of Llandaff, archdeaconry of Monmouth and the deanery of Usk. In the early 1860s, the area of the parish was 4,092 statute acres, and the rateable value £6,663. Edward Francis Bluett Esq., of Llantarnam Abbey, was the lord of the manor and principle landowner. At Cwmbran (the Valley of the Crow), in this parish, was the extensive iron and wire works of Messrs. Hill and Batt, and Roper and Co., the Patent Nut and Bolt Company, Ltd, and the vitriol works of James Gibbs, Esq. There was also a large brick works belonging to Cyrus Hanson, Esq. The Monmouthshire Railway, and the Monmouthshire Canal intersected the parish. (2) The population in 1861 was 1,301 souls.

In addition to Thomas and John, eight other children were born to Michael and Margaret Fielding. These were Michael, Margaret, Dennis, James, Maurice, Patrick, William and Joseph. At this time, many folk would have a large productive garden in order to supplement their low wages, hence the long gardens which mostly accompanied houses of the Victorian period. So it was not surprising that Michael Fielding became expert at growing vegetables and would for many years be self employed as a market gardener with his quality produce to be bought in the local shops. Around the early age of nine years, John Fielding left school with very little formal education, although there is some documentary evidence showing that he attempted to fill in the gaps in his education later on. It was at this time he commenced work as a labourer and began his long association with the nearby Patent Nut and Bolt Works of Messrs. Weston and Grice.

A few years later, an Irish family by the name of Murphy came to live in a new row of houses near Penywain Road, Cwmbran. Thomas Murphy passed away, in 1872, at the early age of 54 years, and left his wife Julia to bring up their four

Michael and Margaret Fielding

children. Her only daughter Elizabeth, who was born in Ireland, and who would later work as a dressmaker, was to play an important part in the life of the young boy living in the nearby Penywain Cottages. It was this young boy who was destined for immortal fame.

Chapter Two

THE KAFFIR WAR

Exactly why John Fielding suddenly decided to join the Army will never be known or why he used the name of Williams as an alias. There was no national emergency around the time of his enlistment in the regular army, which would have compelled him to assist in the defence of his country's interests. Even the low labourer's wage at the local Nut and Bolt Works was better than the shilling a day he would have received as a private. Examination of court documents for this period shows that he was not in any way in dispute with the legal system. It is always possible that after almost eleven years as a labourer in the Nut and Bolt Works of Messrs Weston and Grice, he thought that a tough army life would be more adventurous and an opportunity to see something of the world. A well rehearsed reason given by his family members in those far off days is that he was too young to join up, yet, official records show that he was in fact of the correct age. Cwmbran folklore suggests that the young man joined under an assumed name so that his father would not be able to trace him, but no reason is given why he was avoiding a confrontation with his father. Possibly, his older brother Thomas, who had been a volunteer in the 6th Monmouthshire Rifle Corps since January 1876, may have influenced him in some way.

For personal reasons only known to himself, the slim young man with a height of around 172cm (5 feet 8 inches) arrived in the market town of Monmouth. On the 22nd May, 1877, he enlisted in the 24th Warwickshire Regiment of Foot, and accepted the traditional shilling that was to bind the bargain between the recruit and the recruiting officer. Such was the positive approach of the army in those bygone days, that whatever name the recruiting Sergeant wrote on the enlistment form, as far as the army was concerned, the recruit would always be known by that name; even if the recruitment Sergeant spelt the name wrongly. The next day, another young man also enlisted in the regular army at Monmouth. Private Joseph Williams started his working life in the Cordes Dos Works in Newport, Monmouthshire, and both became firm friends by the time they were posted together on August 3rd, 1877, to B Company, 2nd Battalion 24th Regiment, which at that time was stationed at Dover Citadel, and later Chatham.

Extracts from the published historical records of the regiment explain how 1395 Private John Williams, and his new found comrades were soon under orders for South Africa:

John Williams (left) as a young recruit

The serious aspect of affairs on the Eastern Frontier of the Cape Colony at the close of the year, led to a call for reinforcements, and on the 28th January, 1878, a telegraphic despatch from the Horse Guards directed the 2nd Battalion 24th to be held in readiness for the Cape...on 1st February, 1878, the battalion left Chatham by two special trains for Portsmouth, where it embarked in H.M. troopship Himalaya, and started next day. The strength embarked was twenty-four officers, eight staff-sergeants, thirty-nine sergeants, forty corporals, sixteen drummers, and seven hundred and forty-six privates.(3)

Among these privates to embark on February 1st, was also to be found a Private William Osborne, 1480, B Company 2/24th, of Blaenavon, who attested at Pontypool on November 28th, 1877. He later remembered distinctly that one of the first tasks for everyone when going on board the old Himalaya, was to empty the ticks (mattress sacks) of old straw, which was then taken to the quarter master for refilling. (4) Although the weather was good, disciplinary problems were bound to very soon emerge with so many men living in the cramped on-board living quarters. On the 11th February, another member of B Company, 662 Private John Murphy, of Newport, was confined and sentenced to twenty five lashes.

On February 27th, 1878, Elizabeth Murphy, a dressmaker, of New Row, Cwmbran, (no relation of the above John Murphy) gave birth to a baby girl, whom she named Ann. No name of the father of the child was registered on the birth certificate, or on the baptism entry.

The history of the regiment continued: After a fine passage, the Himalaya reached Simon's Bay on 28th February, after coaling there, and making good some repairs, it resumed the voyage on 6th March, and sighted East London on 9th March. The day being favourable for crossing the bar, "B" and "C" companies, under Major Dunbar, were landed at once in serf boats. The bar and heavy serf made landing at East London a slow and offtimes dangerous operation, and not until 11th March was the last company got ashore. As fast as trains could be procured for them, the companies were hurried off to King William's Town, where it was concentrated by March 14th. From here it marched to the front.

As it was known to the British, the sixth Kaffir War of 1877-78, was held mainly against the two tribes of the Gaikas and the Galekas. The reasons for the uprising by the natives is obscure in the least, but it was generally believed that the over population of the regions where they existed was a main contributory factor to the war breaking out in the Cape Colony. With only the "red soldiers" of the 1st Battalion 24th Regiment, present at first to deal with these scattered uprisings, it was thought that a great deal of fighting was yet to follow and the supporting 2/24th Regiment would not be long in entering the conflict.

In the only documented interview ever given by 1395 Private John Williams, he states: "We got to South Africa in the beginning of 1878, and remained at

Bailey's Post some time".(5)   The region into which the 2nd Battalion marched is well described in the regimental history:

The tops of mountains are large plateaux, well supplied with grass and water, but intersected by deep ravines and rocky bush. So precipitous is the ground, and so thickly is it wooded, that only on the very verge of a ravine, or kloof, is discovered the unsurmountable obstacle it presents to an advance in some direction, which a short distance off appeared perfectly easy. The slopes of these table-lands were defended by similar obstacles; dense bush, full of rocks, ravines, and trees of enormous growth; the ascent becoming steeper as one advances, until in most cases it terminates in a precipitous face of rock, or krantz, of great height. Few points in these krantzes are accessible to the natives, fewer still to the Europeans. Indeed, the difficulties and intricacies of the country must be seen to be properly understood. However well known the country may have been in former wars, no actual knowledge of it for military purposes was at hand; even the white settlers and their labourers living on the skirts of the forest were ignorant of the main path through it and over the mountains. In fact the rebels (natives) were in vast natural fortresses, where they had ample supplies of wood, water, and grass, beside their store of mealie (Indian corn), which later they sought to replenish by nightly raids on the neighbouring Fingo locations at the foot of the hill. Nor had they any lack of ammunition, as later on they were seen from Mount Kempt actively engaged in drill and target practice.

From the time it landed, the battalion was engaged in marching, patrolling, or waylaying paths leading to the rebel position, up to Sunday, 17th March, 1878, when the General arranged a combined attack for the following day. This particular attack did not meet with any great success. However, a week later another attack was made and General Thesiger, from Mount Kempt, witnessed the operations of "B" and "C" companies, in clearing three separate clumps of bush immediately beneath him. Afterwards he personally complimented them on the "admirable manner" in which the service had been performed.

On 6th April, the rebels were again attacked, and defended themselves well, but were driven from the bush. During the night the rebels broke away in various directions, but about 7 a.m. on the 7th, a body of one hundred and fifty or two hundred being seen passing near Baillie's Grave into the Pine bush, "A", "B", and "C" companies were sent out to intercept them. The Tutu bush was driven and forty Kaffirs killed, among whom were two chiefs. Another who was to share with John Williams the hard life endured by a soldier on active duty, and the same experience that day, was Private James Frowen Williams, of Abersychan. He had enlisted at the age of twenty years, with John Prosser, a friend in the Monmouthshire Militia. Both took the Queen's shilling at the Full Moon Hotel, Pontypool, where they were sworn in by Rev. J.C. Llewellyn, vicar of Trevethin. Private Frowen Williams, belonged to either "A" or "C" company, and in later years gave a vivid recollection of the battle. He told of how they had fought in shirt sleeves and killed the Kaffir chief. In the battle, which raged in the bush, a man named John Collins, of Merthyr, was mortally wounded and Frowen-Williams, with others, helped to carry him deeper into the bush, which was on fire.(6)

In the final combined movement brought against the Kaffirs, the regiment's history states:

> "A" and "B" companies, under Major Dunbar, were actively engaged in carrying some of the Kaffir positions about the foot of Mount Kempt. On each occasion the enemy fled into an accessible bush. On 9th May, these companies again descended from Mount Kempt and drove the bush in the western part of Buffalo Poort.

Private John Williams well remembered this action many years later and spoke of Captain A.G. Goodwin-Austen (whose brother was later killed at Isandhlwana), who was his captain, and Bromhead, his lieutenant. He remembered what he described as a brush with the Kaffirs, and Captain Austen was wounded and went home. "Captain Austen was shot in the loins by a Hottentot, who was up a tree, and we soon settled accounts with him."

"A" and "B" companies were to be stationed at Mount Kempt in May and June, as a deterrent to any further activity by the Kaffirs. At the end of June 1878, the Colonial Government proclaimed a general amnesty.

The operations against the Galekas and other Kaffir tribes had not resulted in heavy casualties. With only one man killed in action, and a few wounded, the main loss was through disease. But, the work had certainly been strenuous, and both battalions earned much praise for their cheerfulness in facing hardships and discomfort, and by their good conduct combined with discipline in the field. General Thesiger, who had succeeded to his father's peerage and become Lord Chelmsford, spoke in the highest terms of both battalions, emphasizing how well the younger soldiers, of whom the 2nd Battalion was in large measure composed, had come through the severe ordeal of hard work in the face of difficult conditions.(7)

Chapter Three

THE ZULU WAR

Sir Bartle Frere, Britain's High Commissioner in South Africa, thought a quarrel with Cetewayo, King of the Zulus, would be an adequate excuse to crush the Zulu empire and subdue the blacks throughout South Africa. A few petty incidents presented themselves, the best being the running away of two Zulu wives, who fled across the border into Natal during July 1878. They were recaptured by the Zulu men, dragged back into Zululand, and executed, according to their customs, within sight of the border guards.

Sir Bartle Frere used this trivial excuse to start a war. Beneath a huge wild fig tree, now a national monument known as the Ultimatum Tree, the Zulu indunas met to consider his conditions. As well as handing over the executioners, and paying a large fine in cattle, they were ordered to disband their army, and to permit all men to marry without the need to 'wash their spears in blood'.

As no reply had been received after thirty days, Sir Bartle Frere officially declared that Natal and Zululand were at war.

Prior to the declaration, the 2/24th Regiment was ordered up country to Natal at the end of July 1878.

Leaving the women and children and heavy baggage behind at King William's Town, the battalion embarked by half battalions at East London on 24th and 26th July, and, after landed at Durban, marched to Pietermaritzburg, arriving there on 6th August. It remained encamped for about three months at Pietermaritzburg, busily employed in drilling and refitting. Several field days took place under the General.

War with the Zulu king Cetewayo being a foregone conclusion, and in point a mere question of time, orders were issued for the troops to move gradually towards the frontier. This was more to allay the alarm among the border farmers than for any purpose of attack, as the preparations for any movement on our side were still very much incomplete.

"B" company, containing Private John Williams and a number of other recruits from the Eastern Valley of Monmouthshire, moved next to Greytown and went into camp about thirty miles south of the Natal-Zululand border. Conditions in the camp for the Cwmbran soldier, and his comrades, are splendidly described by a leading war correspondent of the time:

The camp itself was pitched on a slight hill, about three-quarters of a mile before Grey Town, on the right-hand side of the road, and was very comfortable arranged. Besides the tents of the soldiers, there was a large iron store recently built for the Commissariat and Transport Department. Altogether, there were six companies of the 2/24th, the other two which were at Pots Spruit, from which they were ordered into Grey Town...and Major Harness's Battery of the Royal Artillery, consisting of six guns...The health of the camp was exceedingly good, and only about one per cent. were in hospital. Athletics of every kind were encouraged, and all the men under fifteen years' service ran a thousand yards every morning before breakfast. Although the men were paraded daily, and went through the ordinary drill, they were not overworked, and had plenty of leisure time.(8)

A message came in from the Border that told of Cetewayo calling in his men for the different regiments, and a decision was made to send four companies of the 2-24th to Helpmakaar at once instead of waiting over Christmas Day. The wagons were got ready in good time with serviceable oxen, and headed by their band, the four companies, under Major Dunbar, marched out of town at 11.30 a.m. In a letter to his wife in Dover, Corporal H. Brown, of the 2-24th, gives an indication of the hard marching expected by Private John Williams and the soldiers of the 2-24th.

I received your ever-loving and welcome letter on 23rd December, the one you wrote on the 20th November, and the one you sent Christmas compliments in. I was very pleased to hear from you and to hear that you were quite well in health, hoping that you will remain so. I hope that you excuse me for not writing sooner, for the day after I got your letter we had to go on a march to Helpmakaar, a distance of seventy-four miles, and I can assure you it was a very hard march too the first day. We started from Grey Town at 11 o'clock and we had a hill to go up seven miles long. We had sixteen miles to go the first day, and got to camp about six o'clock p.m. The second day we started about five o'clock in the morning; we went eleven miles, crossed the river Mooi, all down hill, and got there about ten o'clock. We had our breakfast and Christmas dinner after we had crossed, at the other side, a dinner which was not fit for a dog to eat - at least, the meat we had dogs would not eat it; it was bullocks that had died on the side of the road and were then cut up for us. As it said on the card a joyous Christmas you wished me, and I can assure you it was a joyous one; the worst I ever spent in all my born days.

At three o'clock the same day we left the Mooi River, marching twelve more miles, that was altogether twenty-three miles that day; to make it worse we had to go through a wood seventeen miles long. At eight o'clock that night we got to the River Tugela, and it was that dark we could not see one another, and raining in torrents, and we had to sleep on the ground wet through without anything to put under or over us. That was the joyous Christmas I spent in South Africa in the year 1878, one that none of us will forget while we live. We slept that night, got up the next morning at five o'clock and commenced to cross the river at six, and we had not done until four in the afternoon. We then pitched tents and slept there for the night. We started the next morning at four o'clock and went eight miles; halted, had breakfast and dinner, and started again at three, marched ten more miles and got to camp at seven-thirty at Sands Spruit, where there were two thousand native soldiers encamped who are going to fight on our side. We had a rest there next day. Sunday we marched at five and had a worse hill to go up than the one on the first day, but not so long. We got to the camp at Helpmakaar about five-o'clock in the evening and was played into camp by the band of the 1-24th Regiment who were there before us. They had a nice bit of dinner ready for us, and did all the work for us when we got in; it was very good of them for doing it for we were all tired.

This is the worse I have gone through since I got out here, and now we can see the enemy at drill who we are going to fight. All the marching is very bad. I cannot tell you when the fighting is going to commence, but he (Cetewayo) had got until the 11 January to consider if he will come to terms and if not then we shall begin to fight. It is not any use you asking me for money until this is over, for we cannot get anything at all; and you talk about being teetotal, I am forced to be for I cannot get anything out here whatever for love nor money. I don't think we will finish this war so soon and easy as the other, for they are a better lot of men and more of them and they have got rifles the same as we have. I am very sorry to have to tell you that there will be many a poor wife lose her husband and many a father and mother lose their son. I am afraid, but I hope and trust to the Almighty that I shall not be one of them for my own darling's sake.(9)

"B" company moved forward to the front line and arrived at Rorke's Drift on the Natal side of the border. Another of its privates, 1061 John Jobbins, of Pontnewynydd, wrote the following letter to his parents. It was received by his father William Jobbins, the Post boy at the Crown Hotel, Pontypool. This letter also describes the difficult conditions which "B" company were experiencing.

Camp, Rorke's Drift, Jan. 8th, 1879.

My dear Father and Mother, - I answer your most kind and welcome letter, which I received at Maritzburg, owing to our being moved about all over this Colony. The way we are situated is, we are in this place to-day and away to another place to-morrow. We left Maritzburg about three months ago, and then proceeded to Camp Greytown; from there to a place called Helpmakaar, and you will see by my letter we are just now at a place called Rorke's Drift. It is about four miles from King Cetewayo, and they are mustering all the troops they can get together, not only at

1061 Private John S. Jobbins

this place, but just round his country. They allowed him thirty days to come to the terms of the English, and it expires on the 10th of January; so on the 11th the English troops cross the river to go into his country. Dear Father and Mother, I will now describe a small portion of the journey to you. We were getting ready for a rough Christmas enjoyment, and on the 24th of December there came an order to remove four companies of our Regiment up to Helpmakaar, as it was dangerous for the remainder of the English troops. This is the way we passed our Christmas Day: We had to march 23 Dutch miles, and they were pretty long ones. We started at 5 o'clock a.m. on Christmas morning, and marched 13 miles, and then had a halt for about two hours. We then resumed our journey to the river Tugela, and sighted the river three hours before we arrived at the banks, on account of the roads being so winding and bad, and rain having set in, so that the bullocks could not get along with the waggons and baggage. The consequence was that we had to sleep out in the open air without covering, and we could not get anything to warm us. The Regiment was all done up. We could not even get a drink of water to quench our thirst but what was worse than any dirty water you would see running down the streets at home after a dirty lot of washing, and the only means we had of clearing it was by putting alum into it. The men even went for miles to get some water, and then it was not fit to drink. The next morning, God in goodness caused the rain to fall on the leaves of the trees, and it was a great boon to us, for it was more precious to us than beer at the time. If you read the paper you will see this is the Zulu engagement. There is no telling, dear father, when we shall be properly settled, as there is always some quarrel here with these petty chiefs, but this king is properly crowned by our English Government, and if he won't accede to the terms he must expect the result, as the Governor won't be put on one side by him. We arrived at Rorke's Drift on the 6th, and we were allowed one hour for dinner, and mount our duty, which we were on 24 hours, and not even time for a smoke at times; so I can assure you that it is not all sugar out here. According to these country papers, he has three times as many troops as we have, but I think they will be of little use to him, as there will be plenty of us to do for him and put him down. Our General has plenty of work on hand, and he is a fine man to the men under his command. Dear father and mother, I hope your Christmas was more enjoyable than mine, but they gave us a look at one on the 5th of January, and I hope to spend one better next Christmas, and a more peaceable one than the last. I also wish you happy returns of the year and successful ones. I hope you will answer this by return of post, as you must excuse me for not writing before, but I took the first chance I had. I hope this letter will find you in good health, as, thank God, I am well, and if I continue the same until the end of the campaign I shall be lucky, as there are some men suffering with fever and dysentery, but I hope I shall not be troubled with them, as they are very bad on the field. Dear father and mother, everything we require for use is treble the value we pay in England, and when we are settled our pay is not enough, for if we get a pint of beer and a half ounce of tobacco our pay is done; and higher up the country, the volunteers give as much as £2 or £3 for a bottle of brandy - that is up at Utrecht - so they are worse off than we are. We have to give 8s and 9s for a bottle, so it don't come much to our share. My dear father and mother, I shall write as soon as I get another chance; I cannot tell you in this when that will be, as it is very uncertain. Dear father and mother, I would be very thankful to you if you would oblige me by sending my sister Sarah's carte de visite, and also give my love to George, Harry, and sisters Mary Ann and Sarah; tell them all the particulars, and don't forget my brother William, and also my kind love to Mrs Sullivan. If you look in the papers, you will see how we are getting on. We all live in hopes of bringing this to a favourable end both for our Queen and country. The people in this country are very distant people, and especially the whites. They look to us for assistance, and yet they are so miserable that they don't even like to give us a drink of water; and if soldiers by chance get into their place of worship they send them out, and then the chances are, there is a row. But they don't always get their own way, for sometimes they get a snub perhaps from some of the officers. In Greytown the officers allowed our band to play out of doors, and when the commanding officer heard about their stopping the men from going into the churches and chapels he stopped the band until such time as they allowed the men to go into the churches and chapels, and then they were pretty glad to do it. So now, to conclude with my kind and sincere love to my mother, George, Harry, William, Sarah, and Mary, and accept the same from your ever affectionate and loving son

John Jobbins.(10)

The build up of troops at Rorke's Drift, on the Natal side of the Buffalo River, in readiness for the planned invasion of Zululand continued. The little mission station, consisting of only two low buildings which were slightly raised on a ledge of rock, received its name from an Irish trader by the name of Jim Rorke, who had cut away the nearby banks of the Buffalo River to provide an easier crossing for waggons and carts. Tension increased as the deadline of the ultimatum drew nearer. Drill went on regularly every available moment and Zulu scouts could be seen watching the troops' movements at a distance on the hill opposite. Amongst all this activity, 1112 Corporal John Lyons, of "B" Company 2-24th, and a former postman in the Eastern Valley, was writing the following letter to his mother after what appears to be an admonishment from her in a recently received letter. The letter was written at Rorke's Drift.

8th January, 1879.

My Dear Mother,- I received your kind letter; I was sorry to find that my silence caused you so much uneasiness, but you will please excuse me. It is only now that I can see how neglectful I have been; I would not have been so long silent, but the war being over in the Cape Colony, and the troops being called in from the field, a few months passed over in seeking some amusement. Dear Mother, I will write as often as possible, but I cannot help it if you do not hear from me very regularly. I think we are about to commence a harder war than the one just concluded. I told you in my last that we are very close to the enemy's country. We have moved since then, and are now within musket shot of his land. The Buffalo River divides us; we are putting a pontoon bridge across it now, and I think we shall cross over on the 12 inst. We have only seen a few of then moving about on the other side of the river; but I dare say that the day we cross the river, or the day after, we shall be likely to meet some opposition, as they are very numerous. I will now conclude, hoping you are all quite well, as this leaves me at the present. Please give my love to Tom and all enquiring friends. Give my love to Tom Brown and cousin Kate. Accept the same yourself from your affectionate son,

J. Lyons.(11)

As expected, Cetewayo did not reply to the British ultimatum by the 11th January, 1879, and the invasion of Zululand commenced. The British commander-in-chief, Lord Chelmsford, planned for the entry into Zululand to take place at three points along the border, and at each point a column of British troops would cross the Buffalo River. The centre column would cross at Rorke's Drift and under the command of Colonel Richard Glyn, CB. Lord Chelmsford accompanied this column.

On the morning of January 11th, reveille sounded at 2 a.m., and the camp tents were struck and the different regiments were in position to cross the Buffalo River by 4.30 a.m. "B" company 2-24th was to be left behind to guard the drift, look after the pontoons, and garrison the commissariat store and recently converted hospital. Some of "B" company most probably felt aggrieved at not being included in the future fighting force, yet, some would have been relieved at the thought of no more hard marching for a while. However, for the Eastern Valley boys of "B" company, which included Corporal John Lyons, John Williams, John Jobbins and William Osborne, there was plenty to do on that historic morning. In the thick fog and drizzling rain, waggons and oxen and much equipment had to be got across the river on the pontoons, and this work tried to the utmost the powers of all concerned. Yet, despite all the work which still remained at the small garrison, Corporal John (Jack) Lyons still found time to write another letter to his mother in Pontypool.

Camp, Rorke's Drift, Jan. 16th, 1879.

Dear Mother, - I sent you a letter last week in which I mentioned that we are expected to go to war. Our troops crossed the Buffalo, and fighting commenced last Sunday. I was not present at the engagement, but I could hear the firing and see the smoke of the men's guns very plainly. I cannot say how many of the enemy were killed, but they very soon had to run for it. We captured a good quantity of cattle, horses, sheep, and goats, which will be sold and divided among the troops as prize-money, according to the scale laid down. We have got some black men on our side, who I believe fought very well. There were a few killed and wounded among them. As far as I can hear, that was all the loss on our side, except one or two white men slightly wounded. The column will move forward in a few days, and I expect there will be some more fighting. The General is with our column. In the meantime Colonel Wood and Colonel Pearson are moving forward with two more large columns of troops, and I expect they have killed a great many of the enemy and have no doubt captured a few thousand head of cattle. We have not heard anything of them yet, but I will try to send more particulars in my next. Let Joseph Jones's friends know that he is alright. I saw Groves the other day, and told him they were making enquiries about him at home, so I expect he will write soon. I know you will be glad to know that I am quite well at present, and I hope this will find you all quite well. Dear Mother, I have not received all the papers you sent me, so I think you had better not send any more while this war is going on, as papers are very tempting, and they may never reach me. I think with those few remarks I will close now for the present, hoping to hear from you as often as possible. Please give my love to Tom; remember me to Tom Brown, and Kate, and all inquiring friends; and please accept my warmest love from

Your affectionate son,
J. Lyons.(12)

The central column continued and soon encountered some small resistance in the Bashee Valley. After nine days, a steep flat-topped outcrop hill called

Isandhlwana was reached and on a sloping plain beneath this hill, the third column made camp. Reports received by Lord Chelmsford suggested that the main Zulu impi had been found and he, with Colonel Glyn, and about three thousand troops, left camp with the intention of engaging them in battle. By 1.30 p.m. that day, one of the great disasters in British military history had occurred.

At about 2 p.m., Commandant Lonsdale, of the Natal Native Contingency, was quietly returning to camp after unsuccessfully pursuing a mounted Zulu. Feeling unwell, and exhausted, he was slowly jogging along with the sort of lazy perseverance characteristic of a tired traveller. He had crossed the small water wash to the south of the camp, when his attention was attracted by a bullet passing rather close to him, and on looking up he saw a black man, who had evidently just fired. The real truth, was of course, far from his mind, and he merely thought it was one of his own contingent carelessly firing off his rifle, and he pursued his way. To some extent the incident seemed to have woken him up, and, although he saw what seemed to be our own red-coats sitting in groups in and around the tents, he kept his eyes open. When absolutely within a short distance of the tents he saw a great black Zulu come out of one. He was wearing a red coat covered with blood, and held a bloody assegai in his hand. This made him look around more closely, and he saw that black men, and black men only, were the wearers of our red coats. The truth flashed on him, he could read the scowl of hatred on every face, but his self possession did not leave him, for quietly turning his plucky horse "Dot", he galloped off before the enemy were aware of his intentions. A number of shots were fired after him, but by the mercy of Providence he escaped, and was thus enabled to warn the General, and save his life and those with him. Undoubtedly, had such a warning not been given, Lord Chelmsford, accompanied by his staff, and the troops with him, could have walked into a skilful trap thus laid, and, under such circumstances, few would have escaped.(13)

Most of the events of that day is told in the letters of some of the Eastern Valley men who returned to the camp and found the mutilated bodies of well over a thousand men and boys.

The following letter was received by Mr. George Kelly, Cwmbran, from his younger brother, Private 832 Alfred Kelly, C Company 2-24th Regiment. Both were sons of Jerimiah Kelly, an Irishman who had settled in Cwmbran many years before:-

Rorke's Drift, Natal, South Africa,
January 28th, 1879.

My dear Brother, - It is with great pleasure that I forward you these few lines, in hope that you are well. I am glad to state that I still enjoy good health, and hope it will continue so. I wrote you a letter from Greytown about six weeks ago; I trust you received it to hand safe. At present we are on active service; and it is with deep emotion and regret that I have to acquaint you of a very sad disaster to our troops. There were upwards of 900 killed. I will state the facts as briefly as possible. Our column was encamped in Zululand, the territory we invaded; we were about nine miles of the borders, at a place called Isandula; on the morning of the 22nd of this month, six companies of our Regiment, six guns of the Royal Artillery, also a good number of the Natal Mounted Carbineers and Police, and a battalion of the Natal Native Contingent, left camp at daybreak, having been acquainted that the enemy were encamped about ten miles from our camp; we marched about all day, but could find no trace of the enemy; in the meantime, the enemy must have watched our movements, and marched on our right towards our camp; it is believed that they surrounded our camp about two or three o'clock in the afternoon; they were about 15,000 in number; for protection of our camp there were left in charge five companies of the 1-24th and one company of ours, two guns of the Royal Artillery, a few Mounted Police and Carbineers, and a battalion of the Natal Native Contingent, men in hospital, and a number of officers and servants; the way they surrounded our camp was this - they came shouting and yelling, their war-song was exactly the same as the blacks fighting on our side, and, naturally, our troops thought they were the blacks who belonged to us come away back to camp; but I am sorry to say it was not so; every man of ours fought most bravely, against great odds, for three hours, until they were overpowered and every man was killed, with the exception of a few who escaped; the band boys were cut open and hanged by the heels to the commissariary scales and waggon-wheels; all our men, after they were shot, had their bodies cut open. Dear Brother, I can assure you it was a horrid sight to behold; I hope that I shall never witness such again. Everything was ransacked; we lost a million rounds of ammunition. Our tents were burnt. At present we have nothing but what we stand in. There was an orderly sent to get the column to march back with all possible speed to retake the camp, which we did. Everyone was cool and collected, ready to give the enemy a warm reception; there were about 20 shells thrown to the left of the camp; we fired a few volleys, and marched in skirmishing order, with fixed bayonets, ready to charge; the artillery was in the centre; when we got to the camp the enemy had disappeared, but had taken the booty with them; every step we took was over dead bodies; it was heartrending to behold; supposed loss of enemy 3,000; we lost our colours, also the 1st battalions and all the band instruments; we marched this morning to where we are at present, and found they had attacked this place, held by one company of our battalion, who bravely held their own until we arrived, having had twelve hours hard fighting. Dear Brother, we are certain we will come home after this war is over. I hope the Lord will guide me safely through all, so that I may see you all once more. Indeed, dear brother, war at the best of times is most cruel. The 1st Battalion lost five companies, or about 500 men; our loss is estimated at 185, including officers; Artillery, 65 men; leaders of Natal Native Contingent, 84 men; Police and Carbineers, 66 men - which amount to 900 men. The foregoing are white men, exclusive of blacks lost on our side. I hope when I write again to be able to send you a more favourable account on our side. We are determined to have our revenge on the black devils. Now I must draw to a close, with kind love to mother and brothers, yourself and wife. Mind and write, as I am anxious to hear from home.

I remain, your affectionate brother,
Alfred Kelly.(14)

A letter from Private John James. He grew up in Blaenavon and his father was Mr. William James, who lived at the Coed Farm, close to the town.

H. Company, 2-24th Regiment.

Dear Father, Mother, and Sister, - I write this hoping to find you well, as it leaves me first class. I am sorry to have to tell you bad news. Dear Mother, on the 22nd of January we went out at 3 o'clock in the morning, thinking to have an engagement with the Zulus, but while we were out, about 15,000 came on the camp, killed everyone there, and took everything we had. Our loss was frightful; we lost 5 officers, 10 sergeants, 8 corporals, and 159 privates in our battalion; and the 1-24th lost 5 companies; averaging 600 men and 200 volunteers. Our Regiment also lost our colours, band drums, ammunition, and our baggage, and left us desolate in only what we stood upright in. We had to sleep that night among the dead. It was a dreadful sight to see how our men were cut up; but they killed that day 6,000 of the enemy. Two of the little band boys were hung up on the hooks of the weights that we use to weigh the meat on. Dear Mother, after they had done slaughtering there, they went down to where B Company was with the commissariary, and set fire to the place; but our boys had the best of it there: they killed about a 1,000 of them, and our side only had 11 killed and two wounded. They had to fight hard for their lives that night. Will Osborne had a very narrow escape. He sends his love to you; also Ed. Murray, S. Parry, Wm. Davis send their love to you and all friends. Geo. Slasher got killed in the battle. Joe Hartley sends his love to you. Give my love to all friends, and tell them I am still alive and kicking.

Hasten, message, to my mother.
Far across the dark blue sea;
It will fill her heart with pleasure-
She'll be glad to hear from me.

So no more at present. - From your loving son,
John James.(15)

Private William Meredith, 2-24th, of Wainfelin Road, Pontypool, wrote the following to his brother and sister from Rorke's Drift on February 5th, 1879:-

I write you these few lines in the hopes that you are in good health, as it leaves me at present, thank God, considering we had our second fight, in which we got defeated. At our first fight we gained the day, and took a good many head of cattle. But we are properly defeated now; so we cannot go any further until we get more troops from England, we lost so many men at the last battle. We lost 500 men from the first Battalion and 184 from the 2nd. The second is the Regiment that I am in, so don't make a mistake. These are the Pontypool boys that got killed in the battle, Alf Farr, Dick Treverton, and Charly Long. I expect you will see more of it in the papers, but they generally print them wrong out here, and so they will at home. I could describe the battlefield to you, but the sooner I get it off my mind the better. It was a pity to see about 800 white men lying on the field cut up to pieces and stripped naked. Even the little boys that we had in the band, they were hung up on hooks and opened like sheep. It was a pitiful sight. We had to retire, and make our best way to get ammunition. Please let me know, have you sent more than one letter?(16)

A letter from Charles Jones, of Pontypool.

Lower Tugela Drift, Feb 10th, 1879.

Dear Tom, - I am now set down to write these few lines in the hope of finding you in good health, as it leaves me at present, thank God for it. I am sorry to tell you that my regiment has had a severe loss; there are 174 of the men killed. I have just seen the list of the men killed, and I find that poor Dick Treverton is among them. Poor Dick fought hard for his life, but what can a man do when there are fifty fighting him at once? And what could poor Dick do but fight hard, which he did like a soldier and a man? Dear Tom, when I last saw poor Dick, he was well and happy. He was then in Greytown, and I shook him by the hand, but never did think it was the last time. Dear Tom, there are some more that you may know: there are Alfred Farr, Charley Long, Wm. Rees, (from the Race), and Harry Smith (from Sowhill), all killed-killed by savages, as you may say; but I suppose it will be my turn next. I have no more to say at present, but I hope you are all quite well. Please write soon.

Your affectionate brother,
C. Jones.
2nd Squadron Mounted Infantry.

P.S.-Please break the news gently to Mrs. Treverton.(17)

It was to be reported in the February 15th, 1879 issue of the Monmouthshire Beacon, that the disaster to the 24th Regiment had cast a gloom over Pontypool and surrounding district, as there was said to be, from the parish of Trevethin, no less than 136 soldiers in it; and 30 of that number were belonging to the town, and in the 1st Battalion. The thoughts of a number of relatives in the Eastern Valley of Monmouthshire were now beginning to turn to the sad task of claiming from the War Office, the effects, if any, and campaign medals of those that still remained unburied on that sad field of war. Mrs Jane Morris, who lived in Pontypool for many years, was one of these. In 1882, she received £10 from the War Office, made out by her dead son George's pay outstanding on the day of Isandhlwana, and the sale of his personal effects. Bravery came cheap in 1879.

Chapter Four

RORKE'S DRIFT

As darkness quickly fell on the doomed camp of Isandhlwana, Lord Chelmsford ordered the exhausted troops to rest. They settled amongst the dead, and the full extent of the horror would not be known until the morning. Only then, and many months later, would they learn of the bravery, where men fought back to back, with sometimes over sixty cartridge cases found around the small groups of men where they fell. Zulu warriors who took part in the massacre would tell of a tall man, possibly an officer, who made a stout defence at the end. He came out of a wagon and fired so quickly that he was to drive the Zulus in different directions. At first some of the Zulus took no notice; but at last he commanded their attention by the brave way in which he fought; and because he had killed so many. All those who tried to stab him were knocked over at once, or bayoneted; he kept his ground for a very long time and eventually had to be shot. One of the last left alive was a band boy who threw his small sword at a Zulu. He was caught by the Zulus and tossed into the air to land on their assegais. Several of these small band boys had their legs cut off and were hung by their mouths on the commissariat scales, which were used for weighing meat. Almost every dead body had been ripped open with the heart and bowels torn out. Most of the white men had their noses, ears, and other parts of their bodies cut off and thrust into their mouths. Some had had their sides cut open and their hands pushed into the wounds up to their wrists, as the fashion of pockets, in an attempt at some macabre humour by the savage enemy. Each had been made unrecognisable, some decapitated, and the clothes removed from most made even the recognition of rank impossible. These were the horrors that began to reveal themselves as the morning light appeared. During the night, a fire in the distance, thought to be near Rorke's Drift, gave cause for alarm, for not only was there the possibility of finding further atrocities, but, what was left of the middle column was now very exposed, and the loss of the stores at Rorke's Drift would place them, and Natal, in great danger.

The following official account of the memorable defence of Rorke's Drift was made by its intrepid leader, Lieutenant John R. M. Chard, Royal Engineers. To aid the theme of this particular biography, the report is necessarily interspersed with other relevant information received by the author.

Rorke's Drift, Jan. 25.

"My Lord, - I have the honour to report that on the 22nd instant I was left in command at Rorke's Drift by Major Spalding, who went to Helpmakaar to hurry forward a company of the 24th Regiment. I was specially ordered to protect the ponts. At 3.15 p.m. that day I was watching at the ponts when two men came towards us from Zululand at a gallop. They shouted out, and were taken across the river; and I was then informed by one of them - Lieut. Adendorff, of Commandant Lonsdale's regiment, who afterwards remained to assist in the defence - of the disaster befallen at Isandula, and that the Zulu's were advancing on Rorke's Drift. The other, a Carbineer, rode on to take the news forward to Helpmakaar.

. "Almost immediately afterwards I received a message from Lieutenant Bromhead - commander of the company of the 24th Regiment at the camp near the commissariat stores - asking me to come up at once. I gave instructions to strike the tents, and to put all stores into the wagons, while I instantly made my way to the commissariat store, and there found that a note had been received from the third column, stating that the enemy were advancing in force against our post, which we were to strengthen and hold at all costs. Lieutenant Bromhead was already most actively engaged loopholing and barricading the store building and hospital, and also in connecting the defences of the two buildings by walls constructed with mealie bags and waggons. I held a hurried consultation with him and Mr. Dalton, of the commissariat - who was actively superintending the work of the defence, and whom I cannot sufficiently thank for his most valuable services - and I entirely approved of his arrangements. I then went round our position down to the ponts, and brought up with their guard one sergeant and six men, the gear, waggons, & c. I desire here to mention for approval the offer of those pont guards, Daniels and Sergeant Milne, of the 3rd Buffs, who, with their comrades, volunteered to moor the ponts out in the middle of the stream, and there to defend them from the decks, with a few men to assist.

"We arrived back at our post at 3.30 p.m., and shortly afterwards an officer with some of Durnford's Horse came in, and asked orders from me. I requested him to send a detachment to observe the drifts and ponts, and to throw out vedettes in the direction of the enemy, in order to check their advance as much as possible, his men falling back upon the post when forced to retire, and thereafter to assist in the defence. I next requested Lieutenant Bromhead to station his men, and, having seen every man thoroughly knew his post, the rest of the work went quickly on.

[Lieutenant Chard detailed a handful of men to protect the makeshift hospital, and any of the wounded who was fit enough, was given a rifle. One of the patients was Gunner Abraham Evans, "N" Battery, 5th Brigade, Royal Artillery, who was to live the remainder of his life at Spring Gardens, Varteg, near Pontypool. Gunner Evans took up his firing position on the parapet alongside Lieutenant Chard. Private John Williams, with his close friend Private Joseph Williams and Private William Horrigan, a patient, was posted to a distant room of the hospital, which held a door as the only means of exit.]

"At 4.20 p.m. the sound of firing was heard behind the hill to the south. The

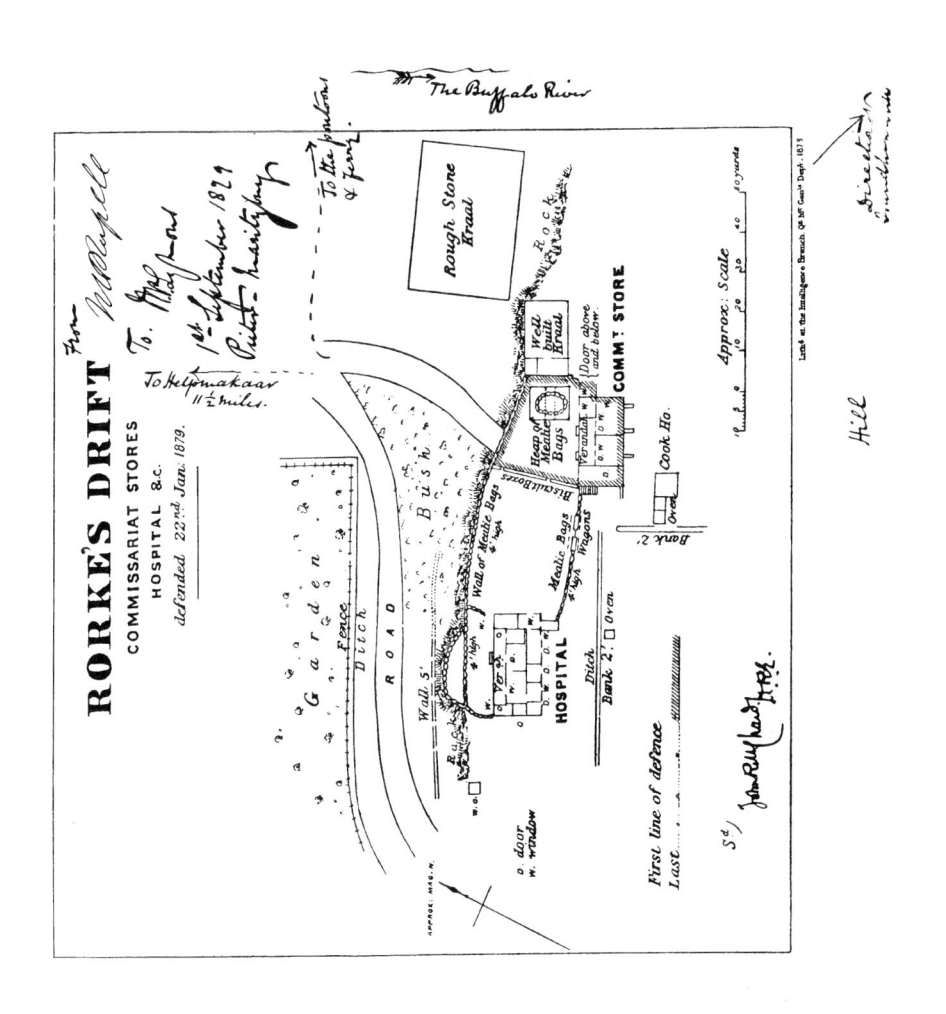

RORKE'S DRIFT
COMMISSARIAT STORES
HOSPITAL &C.
defended 22nd Jan. 1879.

officer of Durnford's Horse returned, reporting that the enemy was now close upon us. His men, he told me, would not obey orders, but were going off towards Helpmakaar, and I myself saw them in retreat, numbering apparently about 100, going in that direction. About the same time, Captain Stephenson's detachment of the Natal Native Contingent left us - as did the officer himself. I saw that our line of defence was too extended for the small number of men now left, and at once commenced an inner circle of entrenchment of biscuit boxes, out of which we had soon completed a wall two boxes high, when, about 4.20 p.m., five hundred or six hundred of the enemy came suddenly in sight around the hill to the south. They advanced at a run against our south wall, but were met by a well sustained fire; yet, not withstanding heavy loss, they continued to advance till within fifty yards of the wall, when their leading men encountered such a hot fire from our front, with a cross one from the store, that they were checked. Taking advantage, however, of the cover afforded by the cook-house and the ovens, they kept up thence heavy musketry volleys; the greater number, however, without stopping at all, moved on towards the left round our hospital, and thence made a rush upon the north-west wall and our breastwork of mealie bags. After a short and desperate struggle those assailants were driven back with heavy loss into the bush around our works. The main body of the enemy close behind had meantime lined the rocks and filled some caves overlooking us at a distance of hundred yards to the south, from whence they kept up a constant fire. Another body, advancing somewhat more to the left than those who first attacked us, occupied a garden in the hollow of the road and also the bush beyond it in great force, taking special advantage of the bush, which we had not had time to cut down. The enemy was thus able to advance close to our works, and in this part soon held one whole side of the wall, while we on the other kept back a series of desperate assaults which were made on a line extending from the hospital all along the wall as far as the bush. But each attack was most splendidly met and repulsed by our men with the bayonet, Corporal Schiess, of the Natal Native Contingent, greatly distinguished himself by conspicuous gallantry. The fire from the rocks behind our post, though badly directed, took us completely in reverse, and was so heavy that we suffered severely, and at six p.m. were finally forced to retire behind the entrenchment of biscuit boxes.

[During this time, Corporal John Lyons, Private John Jobbins, Private William Osborne and Gunner Evans, all men of the Eastern Valley of Monmouthshire, and Corporal Alfred Saxty and Private John Murphy, of Newport, were all fully occupied playing their part in the desperate struggle at the barricades. Both considered to be marksmen, Corporal Lyons was busily firing alongside Corporal William Allen, of Monmouth, when a bullet passed through a small gap between the biscuit boxes and hit him in the neck. The bullet lodged in his back, striking his spine. With his right arm partially disabled, he said, 'Give it to them Allen. I am done; I am dying'; and he replied, 'All right, Jack'; and while speaking to him he saw a hole in the right sleeve of his jacket, and said, 'Allen, you are shot', and he replied, 'Yes; goodbye'. Allen walked away, with blood running from his arm, and he helped to serve ammunition all night. As Corporal Lyons lay wounded, he gave encouragement to the men and was later moved to the inner defence where he received medical attention from Dr. Reynolds, the army surgeon.]

"All this time the enemy had been attempting to force the hospital, and shortly afterwards did set fire to the roof. The garrison of the hospital, defended the place room by room, our men bringing out all the sick who could be moved before they retired. Privates Williams, Hook, R. Jones and W. Jones, of the 24th Regiment, were the last four men to leave, holding the doorway against the Zulus with bayonets, their ammunition being quite expended. From want of interior communication and the smoke of the burning house, it was found impossible to carry off all of the sick, and with most heartfelt sorrow and regret, we could not save a few poor fellows from a terrible fate.

[Private John Williams and his colleagues held the room for more than an hour, firing through the improvised loopholes made in the walls. Their ammunition began to run out and with the Zulus by this time working to break down the door to the room, Private John Williams sought a way of escape to safety for the patients and his fellow soldiers. With the use of an axe, he hacked a hole through the partition wall; which was made of sunburnt bricks of mud. While this was taking place, the Zulus had succeeded in breaking down the door and Private Joseph Williams was fighting desperately with the bayonet to keep the savages at bay. At this point, the bodies of fourteen warriors lay around the doorway before the Zulus eventually seized Private Joseph Williams and stabbed him with their spears before mutilating his body and ripping out his intestines. While this was taking place before the eyes of Private John Williams, he managed to remove the two patients through the hole in the partition wall and to the temporary safety of the next room. Any rush by the Zulus to get through the newly made hole in the partition would have been dealt with severely by 1395 Private John Williams, especially after witnessing the brutal demise of his close friend. This other room was being defended by Private Alfred H. Hook, the hospital cook, and he heard John Williams shout, as he entered the room, 'The Zulus are swarming all over the place. They've dragged Joseph Williams out and killed him.' They were trapped and it was only Private Williams who seemed to quickly grasp the extremely dangerous situation they were in. He hurriedly proceeded to block the hole he had made in the wall with the body of a Zulu who had attempted to follow him, and, as it was only a matter of time before the Zulus would think to break down the door to this room, Private Williams commenced making another hole through the partition to the next room. Through these hastily made means of escape, each incapacitated patient would be lifted. One of these patients, John Conolly, of Pontypool, proved particularly burdensome as he was a heavy man and crippled with arthritis of the knees. And so, only due to the quick thinking of Private John Williams and his bravery, assisted by the courage of the other hospital defenders, were most of the patients brought to safety.]

"Seeing the hospital burning, and desperate attempts being made by the enemy to fire the roof of our stores, we now converted two mealie bags heaps into a sort of redoubt, which gave a second line of fire all along, Assistant Commissary Dunne working hard at this, though much exposed; thus rendering most valuable assistance.

"Darkness then came on. We were completely surrounded, and, after several furious attacks had been gallantly repulsed, we were eventually forced to retire to the middle and then to the inner wall of our kraal on the east of the position we first had. We were sustaining throughout all this a desultory fire, kept up all night, and several assaults were attempted, but always repulsed with vigour, the attacks continuing until after midnight, our men firing with the greatest coolness, not wasting a single shot. The light afforded by the burning hospital proved a great advantage. At four a.m. on the 23rd January firing ceased; and at daybreak the enemy were passing out of sight over the hill to the south-west. We then patrolled the ground, collecting arms from the dead Zulus, and strengthened the position as much as possible. We were still removing thatch from the roof of the store, when about seven a.m. a large body of the enemy once more appeared upon the hills to the south-west. I now sent a friendly Kaffir, who had come in shortly before, with a note to the officer commanding at Helpmakaar, asking help. About eight a.m., however, the British Third Column appeared, and at the sight of this the enemy, who had been gradually advancing towards us, commenced falling back as our troops approached.

"I consider the enemy which attacked us to be about 3000; we killed about 350. Of the steadiness and gallant behaviour of my whole garrison I cannot speak too highly. I wish especially to bring to your notice the conduct of Lieutenant Bromhead, of the 2-24th Regiment, and the splendid behaviour of his company, B, 2-24th; of Surgeon Reynolds in regard to his constant attention to the wounded under fire, assisting them where they fell; of Acting-Commissary-Officer Dalton, to whose energy much of our defences were due, and who was severely wounded while gallantly assisting in the fight; Assistant-Commissary Dunne, Acting Storekeeper; Colour-sergeant Bourne, 2-24th; Sergeant Williams, 2-24th; wounded dangerously, Sergeant Winbridge, 2-24th; Corporal Schiess, N.N.C.; wounded, Private Williams, 2-24th; Private Jones 2-24th; Private McMahon, A.H.C.; Private R. Jones, 2-24th; Private H. Hook, 2-24th; and Private Roy, 1-24th.

The following return shows the total number present at Rorke's Drift on January 22, 1879:- Eight officers, 131 non-commissioned officers and men; total 139. The following is a list of killed:- Sergeant Maxfield; Privates Scanlon, Hayden, Adams, Cole, Fagan, Chick, and Williams, all of the 2-24th; Private Nicholls, Horrigan, Jenkins, 1-24th; Mr Byrne, Commissariat Department; Trooper Hunter, Natal Native Contingent; Trooper Anderson, Natal Native Cavalry; a private of the N.N. Cavalry. Total, 15, and 12 wounded, of whom two have since died, Sergeant Williams, 2-24th; Private Beckett, 1-24th.

"(Signed) John R.M. Chard, Lieut., R.E."

When the enemy passed out of sight in the early morning light, the relief of the men at the barricades was enormous. With no officers present, Private John

B Company 2nd / 24th. Taken after defence of Rorke's Drift.

*1. Lieutenant Gonville Bromhead V.C.., 2. Colour Sergeant Major Frank Bourne. D.C.M... 3. Corporal Alfred Saxty.., 4. Corporal William Allen V.C...
5. Private John Williams V.C... 6. Private Robert Jones V.C... 7. Private Frederick Hitch V.C... 8. PrivateAlfred H. Hook...
9. Private William Jones V.C.., 10. Private John Jobbins.*

Williams pulled out his pipe and lit up. After several deep intakes of the strong tobacco, he passed the pipe to his nearby grateful comrades, who in turn filled their lungs. While waiting for his pipe to be returned, he automatically checked his ammunition pouch and found that he only had two bullets left. The young man had done what was expected of him by the British Army. He, and Private Robert Jones, were probably the only men to have witnessed the brutality of the Zulus and lived. The sight of this was to take a tragic toll on Jones in later years. The Cwmbran man, trapped in the makeshift hospital, had controlled the great fear present in his mind, while doing his full share of the killing with bullet and bayonet. It was only he who had the presence of mind to find a means of escape for the patients and his colleagues. As the sun rose in the African sky, the comrades of John Williams noticed that the hair of the young man had amazingly changed to a much lighter colour, proof of which will be seen in photographs of that time. Although he would later sometimes humorously refer to his hair turning grey at Rorke's Drift, this was the beginning of the legend of Private John Williams' hair turning white overnight.

The garrison at Rorke's Drift had learned of the savagery of the enemy at first hand and before the atrocities of Isandhlwana became well known. Lieutenant Chard gave the number of enemy killed at the Drift as 350. It later became known that another Zulu warrior was to die after the battle had ceased, making the number buried 351. Private Ashton had reported to Lieutenant Bromhead with a Zulu prisoner, only to be told to "get the hell out of here with him." Later, when the shock of the epic struggle began to wear off, enquiries were made to the whereabouts of the prisoner, and Ashton, a lusty Irishman, pointed to a tree from which the Zulu's body was hanging. Not all the dead and dying Zulu warriors were taken away by their fellow warriors. When the relief column arrived at the Drift, a search of the surrounding bush was made and Gunner Abe Evans never forgot the click, as these men fixed bayonets, and there took some revenge for Isandhlwana.

Some of those who took part in the memorable defence of Rorke's Drift were soon to write home in order to allay the fears of their loved ones. The serious wound of Corporal John Lyons, B Company 2-24th Regiment, did not prevent the Pontypool man from somehow sending another communication. This proved to be very fortunate as the Monmouthshire newspapers were soon to mistakenly report his loss in action.

Helpmakaar, February 7th, 1879.
Dear Mother, - I now take the pleasure of writing these few lines, to let you know that I happened to be one of the unlucky ones that got wounded on the 22nd of last month; but thank God that I am getting around favourable again. Dear Mother, the Zulus attacked the camp of the 1-24th on the 22nd and slaughtered five companies of them, and slaughtered one company and a half of the 2-24th. They also attacked the company I belonged to on the same day, at half past 3 in the

The Monument at Rorke's Drift

afternoon. We were stationed at Rorke's Drift, guarding the commissariat and hospital. We were warned that they were going to attack us about one hour before they came. We did the best in our power to make a lagaar to defend ourselves. There were about eighty of us, all told, and we fought like men and kept four thousand of them at bay until morning. Dear Mother, I do not know who all the boys are that got killed from Pontypool, but I know that Farr, the butcher, and young Harry Smith were killed. Dear Mother, I will be able to let you know more in my next letter. I am getting around alright at present. I suppose that I shall be on the road home soon. Give my best respects to Thomas and all my enquiring friends, and you must accept the same yourself.

I remain, your dear son,
John Lyons.

P.S. - Write soon.(18)

Almost a month had passed and the defeated middle column were still at the fortified Rorke's Drift waiting for reinforcements from England. The troops were experiencing difficult conditions by this time, and the weather was extremely wet and cold. Many in the regiment had become sick with fever. A young private by the name of George Weeks, a member of the relief column, wrote home in an attempt to reassure his mother in Pontnewynydd.

Lower Tugela, February 21st, 1879.

Dear Mother,- I now take pleasure in writing these few lines to you in hope that they may find you in good health, as they leave me at the present. I hope the times will soon mend with you, my dear mother. You must not vex about me, but live in hopes that the war will soon be over, so that I can get to your humble home once more. Dear Mother, there is an attack expected here to-night by the Zulus, for they have been firing on the hills around here today, but we are in the fort and ready for them, come what hour they will. It is a month tomorrow since the 24th was cut up, and we have not been able to go near them yet to bury them. We are longing for the reinforcements to get here, as we are surrounded and can't move. Dear Mother, I dare say friends of those poor men that fell here are in great trouble at home now; but I hope you will cheer up and not vex about me, and trust God's will being done. Dear Mother, please write by return of post. I was happy to hear that you enjoyed your Christmas well. I have sent you a picture of a Zulu warrior; you can see his shield and his assegais in front. I must conclude with my warmest love to you, and believe me to remain,

Your affectionate son,
George Weeks.(19)

The difficulties the troops, which included the Eastern Valley men, were being unavoidably subjected to, are made even more obvious in the disgruntled letter from another member of the relief column, nineteen year old Private Henry Moses, 24th Regiment. He was to later live, and die, in Wern Road, Sebastopol, a small village found on the outskirts of Pontypool.

I take pleasure in writing these few lines to you, hoping to find you well, as I am, so far. I know what soldiering is now. We marched 200 miles and haven't had a night's sleep this month. We are in fear every night, and have had to fight the Zulus, who come on us and killed 800 of our men. I wish I was back in England again, for I should never leave. It is sad times here, and we are on watch every night with our belts buckled on and our rifles by our sides. It is nothing but mountains here; all biscuits to eat. Dear father, and sisters, and brothers, goodbye. We may never meet again. I repent the day that I took the shilling. I have not seen a bed since I left England. We have only one blanket, and are out every night in the rain - no shelter. Would send you a letter before but have had no time; and now, you that are at home stay at home. Goodbye, if we never meet again, and may God be with you. Give my love to all friends; and how is Billy and Tim?(20)

Through the newspapers, the people of Natal became very much aware of the bravery of all the defenders of Rorke's Drift and their prevention of Zulu raids in other parts of the colony. Knowing the difficulties they were now experiencing, and as a small token of their appreciation, the inhabitants of Pietermaritzburg subscribed £150 towards the cost of clothing, pens, ink, paper, matches, pipes, and many other small items. These made life more tolerable for the remaining short time they were to stay in the place, which would often be brought to mind during the remainder of their lives. Corporal John Lyons was already on his way home, and experiencing the fame which was to remain with all of them, as they were feted throughout their lives.

In another letter to his mother Corporal Lyons either wrote or had someone to assist him with the following:-

Ladysmith, Feb. 23rd, 1879.

My Dear Mother, - You will be glad to hear that I am still in the land of the living, and in every way likely to get over my wound, which is much to be thankful to God for; and before long, if all goes well, I shall be on the road home. Since I wrote to you we have shifted sixty miles further down country. We came in waggons called ambulances, and I bore the journey surprisingly well. The people here are very good, and such little delicacies as rice puddings, sago, fruit, and other things are sent in every day to the sick and wounded. The ladies of the town also come in and visit us pretty often, and are always ready to send us anything we ask for. My dear Mother, you would think this is a strange town if you were to see it; there are not two houses standing together; they are all what is called self-contained, and most of them stand in their own garden. The inhabitants are mostly English and Dutch. We expect to move further down country in a few days. And now, my dear Mother, give my kind regards to all enquiring friends, and no more at present from your ever loving and affectionate son.

John Lyons.(21)

John Lyons did not convey to his family the true extent of his injury in order not to alarm his mother. He had in fact lost almost all the use of his arms and whenever he moved his head he had to have someone to help him to do so. An exploratory operation performed on January 27th, at Helpmakaar, to find and remove the bullet in his neck almost ended tragically and it was only artificial respiration that saved his life. While still suffering great pain in his arms, he was again operated on at the Base Hospital at Ladysmith. The delicate operation was performed this time without the use of chloroform and Lyons bore the excruciating pain of the procedure without the slightest murmur. Dr Blair Brown successfully traced the line of the bullet and enucleated an ordinary round bullet, with a rather long rough process extending from its smooth surface. In a few days the pain entirely disappeared from his arms, but his right arm did not function the same as before the injury. The complicated surgical notes of the operation was later published in the Lancet.

The 2nd Battalion remained at Rorke's Drift until the middle of April. During this time, the weather had been extremely wet and cold and the ill equipped troops were to lose one officer and twelve men through sickness. In April, four companies moved to Dundee and was shortly followed by B company, who came up from Rorke's Drift to Kopje Alleine for duty on the line of communications. Although these companies were exposed to attack, the Zulus made no attempt to raid the posts.

These difficult times were briefly forgotten by some when a supplement to the London Gazette announced, under date "War Office, May 2nd," that the Queen had been graciously pleased to signify her intention to confer the decoration of Victoria Cross on the undermentioned officers and soldiers of her Majesty's army, whose claims have been submitted for her Majesty's approval, for their gallant conduct in the defence of Rorke's Drift, on the occasion of the attack by the Zulus, as recorded against their names, viz:-

Lieutenant (now captain and Brevet Major) J.R.M. Chard, of the Royal Engineers; and Lieutenant (now captain and Brevet Major) G. Bromhead, of the 2nd Battalion 24th Regiment. - For their gallant conduct at the defence of Rorke's Drift, on the occasion of the attack by the Zulus on the 22nd and 23rd of January, 1879. The Lieutenant General commanding the troops report that, had it not been for the fine example and excellent behaviour of these two officers under the most trying circumstances, the defence of Rorke's Drift would not have been conducted with that intelligence and tenacity which so essentially characterised it. The Lieutenant General adds, that its success must, in a degree, be attributed to the two young officers who exercised the chief command on the occasion in question.

Private John Williams, 2nd Battalion 24th Regiment. - Private John Williams was posted with Private Joseph Williams and Private William Horrigan, 1st Battalion 24th Regiment in a distant room of the hospital, which they held for more than an hour, so long as they had a round of ammunition left. As communication was for a time cut off, the Zulus were enabled to advance and burst open the door; they dragged out Private Joseph Williams and two of the patients, and assegaied them. Whilst the Zulus were occupied with the slaughter of these men a lull took place, during which Private John Williams, who, with two patients, were the only men now left alive in this ward, succeeded in knocking a hole in the partition, and in taking the two patients into the next ward, where he found Private Hook.

Private Henry Hook, 2nd Battalion 24th Regiment. - This man, together with Private John Williams, one working whilst the other fought and held the enemy at bay with his bayonet, broke through three more partitions, and were thus enabled to bring eight patients through a small window into the inner line of defence.

Private William Jones and Private Robert Jones, 2nd Battalion 24th Regiment. - In another ward, facing the hill, Private William Jones and Private Robert Jones defended the post to the last, until six of the seven patients it contained had been removed. The seventh, Sergeant Maxfield, 2nd Battalion 24th Regiment, was delirious with fever. Although they had previously dressed him they were unable to induce him to move. When Private Robert Jones returned to endeavour to carry him away he found him being stabbed by the Zulus as he lay on his bed.

Corporal William Allen and Frederick Hitch 2nd Battalion 24th Regiment. - It was chiefly due to the courageous conduct of these two men that communication with the hospital was kept up at all. Holding together at all costs a most dangerous post, raked in the reverse by the enemy's fire from the hill, they were both severely wounded, but their determined conduct enabled the patients to withdraw from the hospital, and when incapacitated by their wounds from fighting they continued, as soon as their wounds had been dressed, to serve out ammunition to their comrades during the night.

Dr. James Henry Reynolds, James Langley Dalton, Acting Assistant-Commissary, and Corporal Ferdnand Christian Schiess, Natal Native Contingent, were also to be gazetted for the award of the Victoria Cross. Altogether there were eleven Victoria Crosses won at the epic defence of Rorke's Drift, the highest for a single action in the history of the award.

The young soldiers holding the rank of private, and mentioned above, had given little thought to winning their country's highest award for bravery. Private Hitch, who had accompanied Corporal John Lyons back to this country and was with him in the Royal Victoria Hospital, Netley, at the time of being told of the award, was quite overcome with emotion. No record exists as to the reaction to the news of the award by 1395 Private John Williams, of Cwmbran. Bromhead, Hook, and Robert Jones were to receive their award in South Africa, but due to suffering quite badly with a fever, Private John Williams had to wait ten months for the opportunity to be presented with his medal and was in fact the last of the eleven recipients to receive the highest award.

The 2nd Battalion 24th Regiment were puzzled and naturally very much aggrieved at being left behind when Lord Chelmsford commenced his second advance into enemy country on May 29th, 1879. The old soldiers and the now well seasoned men, who had not only the experience of the late Kaffir War, but who also showed what a small number of well handled men could do at the never-to-be forgotten defence of Rorke's Drift. These men, very much to their disgust, were broken up into detachments on the frontier, and occupied with such odd jobs as cutting wood, loading and unloading wagons, etc. They also had the additional humiliation of seeing preferred before them, and passing to the front, the newly created 1st Battalion. This had been reformed since Isandhlwana, and its recruits consisted of strangers, mainly guardsmen. Considering, not six months before, Lord Chelmsford admitted that "these men not only saved the middle column but also the entire colony", and also adding that he "could not find words to express his admiration of their conduct", it does seem hard that the 2nd Battalion were not allowed to avenge the death of their comrades in the old 1st Battalion. It is possible, their over keeness to do this might have resulted in the decision to exclude them from further participation.

Lord Chelmsford began his second invasion of Zululand and his goal was to destroy the royal village at Ulundi. With his troops formed in a hollow square, he halted about 500 metres from the royal kraal and waited for the expected attack. Mr George Purnell of 15, Bridge Street, Pontypool, and, who was a boilermaker for 46 years at the Panteg Steelworks, Sebastopol, near Pontypool, gave a lucid account of the battle many years later.

"I took part in the Ulundi battle on July 4th, when Lord Chelmsford decisively defeated the Zulus in the last battle of the campaign. It lasted two hours and twenty minutes. We had two gattling guns, which were being worked by blue jackets [naval contingent], and so strong were the Zulu reserves that as soon as one body of them were mowed down there was another to take their place. It was like a reaper mowing down wheat. At length the Zulus tied bits of white rag to the end of their assegais and gave in. Lord Chelmsford ordered them to bring their cattle into camp. This was done, the cattle were sold, and each man's share of the prize money was 11s 8d. Officers had double shares."(22)

After Cetewayo's capture had completed the work at Ulundi, the 2nd Battalion 24th Regiment learned that it had been selected for an expedition in the Transvaal, but orders arrived for its transfer to Gibraltar, and so in September it left Ultrecht, where it had been concentrated, for the coast. Comments on the long march was given by George Purnell, of Pontypool.

"We then worked our way back down country. Each man had arrears of pay to draw, and it was thought that if we went back home and drew the money it would cause a great deal of drunkenness, crime, and breaking barracks. So a marquee was erected and filled with barrels of beer, which was sold at 1s a quart".

A march of 250 miles brought them to Pietermaritzburg, where a great welcome awaited "the battalion that had saved Natal". James Dalton V.C. was among the spectators in Church Street as B Company marched through. Upon recognition of their comrade of Rorke's Drift fame, B Company instantly raised an enthusiastic cheer.

Within reach of Durban, an invitation by the Mayor and Council to its citizens to join them in bidding the Heroes of Rorke's Drift 'Farewell' was eagerly and heartily responded to. Colourful bunting floated from the front of buildings in West Street, and all the flag-staffs in the town were prepared in honour of the occasion. The streets were thronged with lively groups of people in holiday attire, who, as noon drew near, made their way towards the Market Square. At five minutes to twelve the train punctually arrived at the West-End Station, every truck filled with men belonging to the gallant 2-24th. As they came into sight, they were greeted by cheers from the spectators who had chosen to wait at the station. When the train halted, the men quickly leapt out of the trucks and formed up outside the station, and the march to Market Square began, headed by the drum and fife band. Immediately behind the band came B Company, the Rorke's Drift heroes, with the other companies following. The march passed down West Street, with the sides lined with spectators, and every door and window, or any other vantage point fully occupied. Waving of hats and coloured handkerchiefs, and frequent cheers greeted them as they advanced, and many followed on foot or horseback to the rendezvous on the Market Square. A large concourse of people had assembled here and a platform was in position in front of a large marquee, gaily decorated with flags. As the men of the 24th filed in upon the parade ground in front of the platform, they were preceded by the stirring music of the drum and fife band, and cheer after cheer greeted them. The staff of the colours surmounted by the Royal Crown and Lion, with the ragged case, but bare of the colours lost at Isandhlwana, was very noticeable. When the platform was fully occupied and the proceedings about to commence, Lieutenant-Colonel Dunbar dismounted from his splendid charger, and gave the order allowing the men to advance close to the platform, thus allowing all of them to clearly hear the address about to be read. Among the 341 men of the 2-24th Regiment were fifty three of the gallant defenders of Rorke's Drift, which included Privates John Jobbins, William Osborne, and John Williams, V.C. Prominent at the front of the men was the recently promoted Major Gonville Bromhead, wearing, nearly hidden by a sash, the Victoria Cross.

The Mayor gave a short address to the assembly in front of the marquee, already prepared with a light refreshment of bread and cheese, with beer. This was followed by the Town Clerk reading a commemorative address which was to be preserved in the archives of the Regiment. At the close of the main proceedings, each of the Rorke's Drift heroes were called forward and presented with an envelope containing a handsomely printed copy of the Address. As each V.C. man came forward he was deservedly greeted with three cheers. (23)

When B Company boarded ship that very same day, each man had in his kit bag, a bible, which they would treasure for the remainder of their lives. Presented by the ladies of Durban, a philanthropic group, each was signed by a 'Miss Wilkinson'. The other memento, the beautifully inscribed scroll, contained the following kind words:

The Officers, Non-Commissioned
Officers and Men of the 2nd Battalion of
H.M. 24th. Regiment.

 As the time has now arrived when you must take your departure from this Colony, We, the Mayor and Town Council, as representing the Burgesses of Durban, Natal, cannot allow you to leave the land whose frontier your heroism has kept inviolate, without delaying your footsteps for a moment upon the shore, while we place upon enduring record this expression of our admiration of your deeds, and of our lasting gratitude to you, for the heroic services performed by you in the defence of this Colony when menaced by an invasion of overwhelming numbers of Zulus on the night of the 22nd January 1879.
 It is not yet a year since, in the shadows of the evening, a company of your Regiment saw approaching from the slopes of the Buffalo River the darkest cloud of invasion that had ever lowered over the wide frontier of British Dominion in Africa.
 The storm which then gathered around you, held in it all the fierce power caught from a recent victory gained over your brethren who had fallen fighting at a vast disadvantage on the sad and fateful field of Isandhlwana.
 Reckless of loss, confident in its numbers and strength, that wild wave of savage invasion burst upon your hastily improvised defences, and surged against the scanty defenders as the sun went down, all through the night, the savage but dauntless foe renewed again and again his attempts to break your line, a line which was weak in all save courage, loyalty and duty. No need for us to repeat now the story of Rorke's Drift.
 As the daylight faded away above the heights of Helpmakaar, it left you simple and untried soldiers, holders of an unknown post, when daylight broke again over the Zulu hills, Rorke's Drift had become a name of pride to those who speak the English tongue over the earth, and each and all of that little garrison had become Heroes.
 Out of the gloom of a great disaster the star of your victory shone resplendent, and Natal, saved by your heroism, dried the tears of her anguish in the glory of your victory.
 Take then, Officers, Non-Commissioned Officers and Soldiers of the 2nd 24th Regiment, the thanks which we Burgesses of Durban, and Colonists of Natal heartily offer you.
 Wherever your future fortunes and the destinies of the Empire you serve may call you, be assured you will carry with you, the honour, the admiration and the gratitude of those who now bid you
Farewell!

Durban	H.W. Currie
Port Natal	Mayor
January 13th 1880 (24)	

Chapter Five

FOR VALOUR

Durban and the vast country of South Africa were left behind as the 2nd Battalion took to the high seas on board the troopship Orontes for the voyage to Gibraltar. Many had left comrades to their eternal peace on the slopes of Isandhlwana mountain or on the bank of the Buffalo River, at the little mission station of Rorke's Drift. The men of the 2nd Warwickshire Regiment of Foot would never forget the part they played in this short passage of history, and for many, a toll in poor health would be extracted in the years that followed. As the troops breathed in the welcome sea air and enjoyed the respite from danger, which the voyage provided, John Fielding, alias John Williams, probably gave thought to his brave young comrade, Joseph Williams, whom he would never forget, and who would never return to his home in Newport, Monmouthshire. If he had survived the Zulu onslaught, he would have certainly received the Victoria Cross. His name appears on the memorial at Rorke's Drift, and when Queen Victoria forwarded a letter of condolence to his father in Newport, Monmouthshire, it was accompanied by a sum of money as an act of grace for "so brave a son."(25)

Garrison duty at Gibraltar was a good management decision by senior army personnel and gave the opportunity for an exhausted Battalion to recover. It was during the six month stay on the "Rock", that John Fielding experienced several important events, and one in particular shaped the rest of his life. Of the eleven Victoria Crosses awarded for the defence of Rorke's Drift, ten had already been presented, either at home or in South Africa. Due mainly to illness and lack of a suitable opportunity, the first official intimation that the eleventh award was about to be made, appeared in the following:

General Orders   *26th Feby. 1880.*

1   *Notification has been received from the Quarter Master General that H.M.S. "Himalaya" may be expected here on Monday the 1st March.*

2   *Lieut. Verschoyle 46th Foot, having arrived here from leave of absence is taken on the strength of the garrison, and attached to the 79th Foot, from this date, until the arrival of the Corps.*

3   *The Division will parade on Saturday the 28th Inst: at the Alameda at 3.30 p.m. to witness the presentation of the Victoria Cross to Private John Williams 2/24th Foot.*
    After the General salute and riding down the line, his Excellency the Major General will take command.

    Dress - Review Order.
    Staff - Review Order.

1st Brigade	*2nd Brigade*
Col: Macdonell 11 H.L.I.	*Col: Glyn R.B.*
Commanding	*Commanding*
Capt: Heldyard. Bde Major.	*Capt: Fielden. R.A. Bde Major.*
R.A.	*93rd*
R.E.	*71st*
79th	*R.Bde.*

    The 2/24th Foot will act independently.
    Line of quarter Columns at 6 paces interval between battalions - 12 paces between the inner flanks of brigades, and the 2/24th which will be in the centre between brigades.

R.A. R.E. 79th.   *2/24th*   *93rd, 71st, R.B.*
    The battalions including R.A. and R.E. will each stand 20 files, excepting the 24th; which will be "As strong as possible," and be formed up in Quarter Column of double Companies.

    Brigade Majors, Adjutants and Markers, will be on parade at 2.45 p.m.

    The R.A. and each Infantry Battalion (except 2/24th) will in addition furnish a company of 20 files to keep the ground under the direction of the Town Major.

    Heads of departments are invited to attend; they will take post at the Saluting Colour,
        By Command,
               signed F. Solly Flood. Col.
               A.A.F.(26)

The unique presentation of the Victoria Cross is the supreme award for valour. It is a decoration, equally available to all ranks, which is awarded only for individual acts of courage 'in the presence of the enemy'. Whatever mechanism of the mind comes into play at a time of great danger, it can never be doubted, even by the individual himself, that a quality is present which enables a person to triumph over his own tremendous fear, and risk his life for others. The medal, a small bronze cross weighing a little over three ounces in weight, and costing only a few pounds to make, is cast in a rather solid Victorian style with little pretensions to elegance. What makes this medal so special are the qualities to win it are so rare, and the few who do win it will only do so after the most searching enquiry into the circumstances of the action for which it has been recommended. Queen Victoria took a great interest in the inception of this award, and it was she who made the important suggestion that the motto should read 'for valour'. Her further remarks led to the thought that it would be fitting to take the bronze from the Russian guns captured at the fall of Sebastopol. These Russian guns, which, incidentally, were made in China, subsequently had the cascabels (the knobs on the breech end of the cannon) sawn off and from which the first group of medals were produced. This gun metal was to be sufficient to meet the needs of the production of the medal up to the time of the Falkland conflict. On June 26th, 1857, a grand parade was laid on in Hyde Park for the first ever presentation of the

Russian gun captured at Sebastopol and presented to the ancient borough of Monmouth. To be seen at the Royal Monmouthshire Royal Engineers (Militia) Regimental Museum, Monmouth.

Victoria Cross, each with the recipient's name engraved on the back. Each recipient also received the small pension of £10 each year. And so began the epoch of the Victoria Cross which was about to engulf a young man from the quiet village of Cwmbran, found at the lower end of the Eastern Valley of Monmouthshire.

Although general orders stated that the presentation of the Victoria Cross to Private John Williams would occur on the 28th February, 1880, and the Governor and Commander-in-Chief, Gibraltar, the General Lord Napier, who would by right perform the ceremony, the only journal found by the author which reported the unique occasion, the Graphic, held the following account: For his deed of gallantry Her Majesty Queen Victoria was pleased to confer the Victoria Cross, and, as far as Private John Williams was concerned, the presentation took place at Gibraltar on March 1st 1880, by Major-General Anderson, Acting Governor, and Commander-in Chief of Gibraltar.

Gibraltar - Presenting The Victoria Cross to Private John Williams for Bravery at the Defence of Rorke's Drift.

After reading the documents recounting why the decoration was bestowed His Excellency addressed Williams in a brief soldierly speech, and then, having dismounted, himself affixed the decoration to Williams' tunic. After this the latter rejoined his Battalion (2nd 24th) amid the cheers of numerous spectators who had assembled at the Alameda Parade Ground and about the Heathfield Monument to witness the ceremony.(27)

The accompanying engraving is from a sketch by Mrs. A.E. Pearse, wife of Major Pearse, 76th Regiment, Deputy Assistant Adjutant-General, Gibraltar. (28)

In July 1880, six months after the arrival of the 2nd Battalion at Gibraltar, the news of the disaster at Maiwand in Afghanistan brought orders for it to prepare for embarkation to India. There was just a little time before its departure for the important presentation of the new Colours to replace those lost at Isandhlwana. This is witnessed by the following General Orders:

General Orders   5.8.80.

1   The presentation of new Colours to the 2/24th Regt. will take place tomorrow afternoon at the Alameda.   The Battalion will be formed in line, facing West, at open Order at 6 p.m. for the reception of the General Commanding.   The Revd. W.H. Bullock, M.A. Senior Chaplain to the Forces will be so good as to attend.   Each of the other Infantry Battalions in Garrison will furnish as party of 20 files under an Officer to keep the ground under the direction of the Town Major.
    Dress (including staff) Review Order.   All Officers and soldiers present as spectators will appear in the same order of dress as the troops.

By Command
F. Solly Flood, Col.
A.A.S.(29)

The Queen had intended to present the Colours herself, but it became impossible to send a Colour party back to England for the purpose and by Her Majesty's orders, the Governor of Gibraltar, Lord Napier of Magdala, made the presentation. This was on August 6th, 1880, and after the Colour pole and crown, all that remained of the old Colours, had been trooped, the new Colours were duly presented. The Governor spoke in the warmest terms of the regimental history and achievements, and in particular of the defence of Rorke's Drift and its well won V.C.'s. A week later the battalion embarked on H.M.S. "Orontes", reaching Bombay on September 1st, after a rapid passage. It was at once sent up to Poonah, but Lord Roberts had already relieved Kandahar and inflicted a decisive defeat on the Afghans. Accordingly, the 2nd Battalion, instead of being sent up to the Frontier, was diverted to Secunderabad, and arrived on September 16th.(30)

This station was fairly healthy, and the officers found sport quite easy to obtain. In July 1881, while at Secunderabad, the Battalion received orders that the time honoured numerical titles of the Infantry of the Line were to be discontinued officially, and that all regiments were to be known henceforth by their territorial titles only. The Twenty-Fourth, however, was to change the title of "Second Warwickshire" given to them in 1782 for that of the "South Wales Borderers".(31)

1395 Private John William, V.C. and also holder of the South Africa Medal with clasp 1877-8-9, was to remain at Secunderabad, India, until his service time expired.

Chapter Six

THE VALLEY OF THE CROW

The population of the village of Cwmbran continued to grow by the beginning of the 1881, and so, a shortage of houses became very apparent, with the few new rows of houses not meeting the requirements of the influx of workers. Around this time, a regular supply of good clean water did not exist, and there was a need for effective sanitary conditions, but the Local Board soon improved these amenities. The arrival of further industries in the district made the prospect of obtaining regular work more likely, and, compared with many other places, it could be said that Cwmbran had progressed into a pleasant place to settle during the early eighteen eighties.

Many of those who took part in the hard campaign in South Africa returned to Great Britain by this time and had completed their contract with the British Army, or bought themselves out of the service. Corporal John Lyons returned to Pontypool on furlough at the beginning of September 1879, and was feted by the 2nd Adm. Battalion of the Monmouthshire Rifle Volunteers, of which he had been a member before joining the regular army. After a great deal of publicity, and through the influence of a Major Phipps, he left the army and the town to become a commissionaire in London. Before leaving Pontypool at the beginning of December 1879, a couple of sovereigns were handed to him as a parting gift from a few friends.(32)

The British Army senior staff continued to worked hard to maintain confidence in their fighting force and to improve enlistment. This was witnessed in the Eastern Valley of Monmouthshire during August 1882, when, after spending a week under canvas at the Polo Ground, Pontypool Road, the camp of the 3rd Mon. Rifle Volunteers, experienced the daunting prospect of annual inspection on their last day. A large crowd assembled to watch the proceedings which commenced at eleven o'clock before Colonel Glyn, C.B., the former leader of the centre column from which four Pontypool men had met their deaths on the slope of the Isandhlwana mountain. At half past two in the afternoon the battalion paraded for general inspection. Colonel Burton was in command, assisted by Captain and Adjutant Browne, V.C. The battalion wheeled into line, and Colonel Glyn, accompanied by Major Bromhead V.C., aide-de-camp, rode forward and received the general salute. Following a minute inspection of the lines by these heroes of the Zulu War, a number of movements were executed, after which Colonel Glyn addressed the battalion, saying he was very pleased with all he had seen.

By the summer of 1883, Private John Williams V.C., still stationed in Secunderabad, India, completed his six years service in the British Army and decided not to sign on for a further tour of duty. He returned home in October, and although some of the other heroes made a secret return home to avoid any welcoming reception, the return of the Cwmbran man was not only quiet but unusual. Although there is evidence that John Fielding could write, he never wrote home to his family and they were unaware of his intended arrival, or, due to his alias, his heroic deeds in South Africa. After six years of life in the service of his Queen and country, the mere youth who took the shilling in Monmouth had gained weight and matured into a battle hardened veteran. Few would have recognised John Fielding as he sat in the railway carriage pulled by the locomotive that tackled the gentle incline of the lower Eastern Valley. Unknown to the young man, he had boarded the through train which ran along the lower line and which is still present as the Newport, Abergavenny and Hereford Railway. This railway line actually passed the large garden at the back of his home in Grange Road, and the young man had intended to leave the train at the nearby lower Pontnewydd Railway Station. When the train did not stop at Llantarnam Station, the annoying thought of the long walk from Pontypool Road Station must have entered his mind. As he stood looking at the familiar views through the open carriage window, he possibly wondered if he would catch sight of his father tending his much loved garden or any other members of his family at the back of the family home. Perhaps due to a railway signal at the temporary stop position, the train slowed down and John Fielding grabbed his chance. Out of the window went his kit bag and tumbled down the embankment. Soon to follow was the owner, who picked himself up and walked into his father's well tended large garden. With a story to tell, which would take a lot of believing, John Fielding was home. To be sure, if known, his arrival would have been signalled by some large demonstration of welcome by the people of Cwmbran. Yet, with the already characteristic modesty he was to show for the remainder of his long life, he informed no one of his home coming and the honour which the village folk would no doubt have paid him was to be dispensed with.

Transferred to the Army Reserve, the young man soon settled well into civilian life. He found work as a labourer and began to be seen courting Elizabeth Murphy, a twenty five year old spinster and dressmaker. Both at this time lived in the small village of Pontnewydd, found alongside Cwmbran, and the pretty young woman had a small daughter of six years of age, who went by the name of Annie Murphy. In less than six months following his discharge from the army, twenty six years old John Fielding married Elizabeth Murphy quietly at the Saint Alban's Catholic Church, Pontypool, according to the rites and ceremonies of the Roman Catholics. On the 15th April, 1884, both signed the marriage certificate and the witnesses was his sister and brother-in-law, Margaret and John Crimmins, of

Raglan Terrace, Cwmbran. No newspapers carried a report of the wedding and no letters following his name were to be seen on the marriage certificate.

In 1884, the first death occurred of a member of the élite group of eleven men who had won the Victoria Cross at Rorke's Drift. Ferdnand Christian Schiess, V.C., became an itinerant worker and had hit upon hard times. A passage to England, paid for by public subscriptions, offered some hope for a better future. Unfortunately, his health had already deteriorated, and he did not survive the voyage. He died on December 14th, 1884, aged 28 years, and was buried at sea. Further sad losses followed. In 1887, James Dalton V.C., died in South Africa, aged fifty-three years, and former Corporal William Allen V.C., of Monmouth, died in 1890. Aged only forty six-years, the latter had only partially recovered from an attack of influenza, which had affected many people in the ancient borough town, when further complications set in which proved untreatable. He left a widow and seven young children. A fund set up gave assistance to his family and plans were made to place the children in an Industrial Home. Lieutenant Gonville Bromhead also died at an early age. He had remained in the British Army and attained the rank of Major. While serving in India, he died of typhoid fever in 1891, aged forty-six years.

While living in the area known today as Cwmbran, the ex-private always went by the name of John Fielding. Very few local people in those early days knew of his accomplishment. Alone, he had to come to terms with the trauma of that terrifying night of the 22nd and 23rd of January, 1879, and the possible anxiety of the fact of his fraudulent enlistment in 1877. Similar enlistments received terms of two months hard labour in Usk goal according to local newspapers. All this may have contributed to John Fielding leading a quiet life until the late eighteen eighties. Fame was suddenly thrust upon the young man when he had to serve as a witness in a court case, but, the magnitude of his brave deeds would not become apparent to him until later in life.

By 1891, John Fielding, aged 33 years, and employed as a general labourer, was living with his young family in one of four terraced houses near the Mount Pleasant Inn, Cwmbran. At No.3, Morgan John Street, the local hero enjoyed life with his young family which consisted of Thomas, aged 6 years, and William and Margaret, aged 2 years. Also present in the home was Annie Murphy, aged 13 years and his mother-in-law, Julia Murphy. Two more children, John and Elizabeth, would be born as a result of this happy existence.

Life had become very full for John Fielding, with various military functions keeping him busy. These would be preceded by chaos in the Fielding home as John attempted to dutifully prepare his uniform and accessories for the big occasion. Sometimes he would be presented in the newspapers, as witnessed in 1893. Under the heading "A Rorke's Drift Hero", one of the Exeter newspapers made special mention of the brave deeds of the Cwmbran Victoria Cross man. In the same year he completed his time with the army reserve and discharged with pension. He soon joined "C" company, 3rd Volunteer Battalion, South Wales Borderers, in which he served until 1904, and attained the rank of Sergeant.

Some men said they were at Rorke's Drift but in fact they had never been to South Africa. Some had been at the small mission station with either the middle column or prior to the second invasion of Zululand, but failed to mention that they were not actually at the legendary rearguard action. And some were to impersonate John Williams, V.C. On at least three occasions known to the author, deceitful attempts to take advantage of his fame occurred. Following one occasion, a man was sentenced to fourteen days hard labour at the Tredegar Court for burglary and impersonating the Cwmbran hero. On another occasion, John Fielding was at work in the Cwmbran Nut and Bolt Works, in full view of many of the workforce, when a dastardly deed occurred in the capital city of Cardiff. A splendid umbrella was appropriated without permission from a reverend gentleman, but the 60 year old culprit was immediately apprehended. During his appearance at the Cardiff Court, he informed the magistrate that his name was John Williams and he served at Rorke's Drift, where he received the Victoria Cross. He further stated that he served in the Egyptian campaign being present at the battles of Tel-el-Kebir and Kassassin. His plea also contained the fact that he would lose his army pension if convicted of the charge. The Clerk of the Court hurried out of court to make some enquiries on the telephone and subsequently the slippery character was released with a caution from the magistrate. On this occasion the impersonation had worked, after which the imposter seemed to disappear into thin air. A report of the court case appeared in the newspapers and caused the Cwmbran hero such embarrassment that he, probably with the urging of his work colleagues, had a statement printed in the newspapers explaining that he had no knowledge of the incident.

D. Bell   R. Jones   Col E. S. Browne   J. Hook   F. Hitch   William Jones   J. Williams

John Merriott Chard V.C., the intrepid leader at the defence of Rorke's Drift, died in 1897, aged forty nine years. He had remained in the British Army and reached the rank of Colonel before being found to have cancer of the tongue. His placid manner made him a great favourite of Queen Victoria. Former Private Robert Jones V.C., who had returned to the sick room with the intention of carrying Sergeant Maxfield from his bed, but was only in time to see him being mutilated by the Zulus, died the following year. At the young age of forty-one years, and during a period of depression, he went into a garden with a gun and blew away the back of his head.

By the beginning of the new century, John Fielding, like many others, began to feel the pinch financially. It was no easy matter to clothe and feed six children, and in particular, see that they all had boots to wear. In an effort to alleviate some of the hardships his family appeared to be undergoing, John attempted to begin a new and difficult career as a public speaker. The following announcement and advertisement in the February 15th, 1901, issue of the Pontypool Free Press, hopefully heralded a new direction in the life of the Cwmbran man.

LOCAL NEWS

Patriotic Entertainment. - We have pleasure in drawing the attention of our readers to the fact that tomorrow (Saturday) and Monday evening, is to be produced, at the Town Hall, a wonderful reproduction of the Transvaal War. In addition to the life-like Cinematograph, Mr John Williams, V.C., of Cwmbran - one of the heroes of Rorke's Drift - will, in graphic and dramatic language, illustrate by means of magnificent scenes, where and how he won the V.C. Mr Wade, late of the 19th Hussars (now at the front with General French) will also relate his experiences. We can safely assure our readers that in patronising the Town Hall on either of these evenings, they will enjoy a most pleasurable entertainment. Mr Williams, who will wear his V.C. and other decorations gained by his indomitable courage, will, without doubt, receive a patriotic reception. The public of Pontypool will, undoubtedly, appreciate the endeavours of Mr Wade and others, in alleviating the position of this popular hero.

Town Hall, Pontypool.
Extraordinary Attractions
On Saturday and Monday
Feb. 16th and 18th, A Grand Patriotic
ENTERTAINMENT
will be given In The Above Hall.

Briton Or Boer
Forty Magnificent Views, illustrated by a
Powerful Limelight Apparatus, lucidily described
by Mr Wade, 19th Hussars.

The Defence Of The Hospital
At Rorke's Drift
Dramatically described by Mr John Williams,
V.C., the hero of the memorable defence, where he earned
the
Victoria Cross. Concluded with a
Marvellous CINEMATOGRAPH DISPLAY.

Doors Open at 7.30. Overture at 8.
Admission - 3d, 6d, and 1s.

On Monday Evening the Life and Times
of HER LATE MAJESTY QUEEN
VICTORIA.

On Saturday evening, February 16th, the large room of the Pontypool Town Hall overflowed with interested people and Mr Wade lectured first. Sergeant John Williams V.C., spoke next and briefly described the defence of the burning hospital at Rorke's Drift. Regrettably, owing to the disgraceful noisy behaviour of some of the occupants in the back seats, his words could not be very well distinguished, and persons even in the front seats had great difficulty in hearing him. This traumatic experience made the naturally reticent Cwmbran man realise that professional public speaking was not for him and he wisely distanced himself from Mr Wade, the promoter.

On July 13th, 1901, a sad event occurred at no.32, Llantarnam Road, Cwmbran. Annie Murphy, aged 23 years, died of pulmonary tuberculosis. A few days later, John Fielding registered the death at Newport and signed the death certificate as John Fielding, stepfather, and no V.C. followed his name. No death notice appeared in the obituary columns of the local newspapers and the death would have gone unnoticed by many, but for a small entry by a reporter at the bottom of a page in the South Wales Argus. These few lines appeared the day after the funeral:

> Cwmbran
> Death of Miss Fielding. - Great sympathy is felt on all hands with Private John Williams (Fielding), of Rorke's Drift fame, who has just lost his eldest daughter after a long and painful illness.

As time passed, occasionally someone would ask where were the remaining heroes who had put up such a stubborn and heroic defence at the little mission station of Rorke's Drift. If, in 1904, a person went along to the Nut and Bolt Works, Cwmbran, he may have seen a middle-aged man, not always too strong in health, owing to his exertions on a terrible night some twenty five years before. Here, John Fielding could be found, earning a scanty living working as a nut cutter in order to buy his daily bread. It was the custom at this time for Great Britain to pay her generals a splendid income, and in the end, a good pension, while such working men from the ranks were offered nothing better than the workhouse if they did not survive financially. Yet, when this ordinary working man was attired in his evening apparel, there appeared on his coat that little Maltese cross with its magic words, "For Valour."

For some time it had been felt in the Cwmbran district that the deeds of such a brave hero had long enough gone unrecognised. Accordingly, a movement had been underway for the purpose of recording, in some marked fashion, the exploits of the famous Monmouthshire man. The need for subscriptions soon met with a ready response and on Thursday, September 22nd, 1904, the Cwmbran Drill Hall of C Co., was resplendent with flags and bunting, ready for an auspicious occasion. Shortly before 8p.m., the officer in command of C Company, Captain B.J. Williams, took the chair, supported by Colonel Bradley, commanding officer

Michael Fielding   John Fielding   Margaret Fielding

of the Battalion. Sergeant John Williams V.C., occupied a seat on the right hand side of the Chairman.

The father of the "lion of the evening" was present.

A full muster of C Company attended, whilst a fair number of the Panteg Battery contributed to the event with their presence. The general public attended in good numbers and the hall became comfortably filled by the time the proceedings commenced.

At the outset, the Chairman proposed the toast of "The King," which was drunk with musical honours.   After several musical items, the Chairman said that they had now arrived at the most important item in the evening's programme, the unveiling of the portrait of John Williams V.C. This was to be hung in the Armoury as a fixed memorial to him, as a member of the company. The most important task of the evening fell to Colonel Bradney, who unveiled the portrait amidst loud cheers from all who were present.

At the foot of the portrait appeared the following inscription:-

>Sergeant John Williams, V.C., 3rd Vol. Batt.,
>South Wales Borderers, late 24th Regiment.
>This portrait has been subscribed for by
>Officers, N.-C. Officers, and Men of the C Co.,
>3rd V.B., S.W.B., and also by the inhabitants of
>Cwmbran, as a token of their respect and in
>honour of the heroic conduct on his part during
>the gallant defence of Rorke's Drift., 22nd Jan.,
>1879.

Very conspicuous, and hanging on the wall opposite the new portrait, was a steel engraving of the burning of the hospital at Rorke's Drift. This had been generously given by Mr W.J. Gibbons, Forge Hammer Hotel, Cwmbran.

During his long speech, Colonel Bradney remarked how pleased he was to see Sergeant Williams's father present, and the hero they were honouring that evening was only one of seven sons that Mr Fielding senior had given to their country's service. His eldest son, a sailor, served with Admiral Tryon when the Victoria was rammed and 336 lives were lost. Also, by strange coincidence, Sergeant Williams's son was at that time serving in Beaufort, South Africa, in the same regiment as his father had done, and even more remarkable, the young man was also in the same Company.

Loud cheers greeted Sergeant Williams when he rose to respond, and he thanked all those present for the enthusiastic way in which they had drunk his health. Colonel Bradney had referred to what he had done at Rorke's Drift, but he thought that any of those present, if in his position, would have done the same. It had been said that if a Britisher became cornered he would fight his way out or die. That was what they had done at Rorke's Drift. Continuing, Sergeant Williams said that if they examined the steel engraving on the wall opposite they would notice the Rev. Mr Smith serving out ammunition. Strange to say, although that man was one of the bravest men in the engagement, his services had not even been recognised in despatches. Sergeant Williams concluded his speech amid loud applause.

A splendid musical programme took up the rest of the evening, and the playing of the National Anthem closed the enthusiastic proceedings.

The following year, on March 12th, 1905, Alfred Henry Hook, V.C., succumbed after six months of suffering with Tuberculosis and passed away in Gloucester. Aged 54 years, he had a wife and two young daughters. Private Hook V.C., had served three years and 105 days of his enlisted six years before he

Presentation Photograph
of
Sergeant John Williams V.C. and Sergeant Alfred H. Hook V.C.

The First gathering of The Old Comrades' Club, Oudenarde Barracks Aldershot 23rd - 24th January, 1904 - Fred Hitch V.C., and John Williams (middle right).

purchased his own discharge from the service. Both he and John Fielding had become firm friends by meeting throughout the years at various military functions. The demise of yet another member of the famous eleven who won the Victoria Cross in such desperate conditions was a great shock to the Cwmbran man. The personalities of both men were at times very opposite, with Hook being the more extrovert, as witnessed by his articles in various magazines which chronicled his exploits, and his need to be noticed. John Fielding on the other hand proved to be more reserved, and kept locked in his mind the dark secrets of his part in what happened in the small hospital in 1879. Fred Hitch was the only Rorke's Drift holder of the Victoria Cross to attend the military funeral. His comrade-in-arms, and friend, John Fielding, had great difficulty when writing a letter of condolence to Mrs Hook.

Time very much marched on for John Fielding. Throughout the years, he had dutifully attended many functions, an example of which is a parade in October, 1912. This activity aroused a great deal of interest in the district. Cwmbran, Pontnewydd, and Llantarnam National Reserve took part in a church parade on a Sunday, after about a hundred marchers assembled in the grounds of the Abbey Hotel. They marched through Oakfield and Cwmbran to St. Gabriel's Church, proceeded by the Griffithstown Brass Band, under the leadership of Mr Tom Berry, and followed by the bugle band of the Pontnewydd Church Lads Brigade. With the Cwmbran Fire Brigade, under the command of S.I. Darby, also in attendance, such veterans as John Williams V.C., and Sergeant J. Powell, of the Hussars, turned out with their decorations.

In 1913, two more of John Fielding's comrades of the Zulu War were to pass away. After a short illness, former Private Frederick Hitch, V.C., died, aged fifty-six years, and was buried at Chiswick. John Fielding, of Pritchard's Terrace, Cwmbran, and Frank Bourne, D.C.M., attended the funeral. Not many months later, former Private William Jones, V.C., aged seventy-three years, also died, sadly leaving only Dr. James H. Reynolds and John Williams remaining of the eleven who won the Victoria Cross at Rorke's Drift.

1914 became an horrendous year for John Fielding, beginning with the demise of his father at the end of February. After being very ill for fifteen days with acute bronchitis, Elizabeth Fielding, aged 55 years, of 146, Llantarnam Road, Cwmbran, went into heart failure and died on May 29th, 1914. Her husband John Fielding was at her bedside. Obsequies were quietly carried out and she was buried at St. Michael's of All Angels Church, Llantarnam.

Until Britain entered the First World War on August 4th, 1914, the South Wales Borderers held the regimental record of Victoria Cross holders with sixteen awards, but only two were still living: David Bell, who won his award in the Andaman Islands, and John Williams. The First World War became the greatest bloodbath the world had seen, costing around ten million lives in just over four

John Williams V.C.   David Bell V.C.

years. At the beginning of the war, young men eagerly enlisted 'to fight for King and Country.' A million men came forward by the end of the year, thus making it unnecessary to introduce conscription until 1916. Although still in a state of bereavement, the sense of duty was still very strong in the man who had taken up arms for his country over thirty-five years before. John Williams V.C., of Llantarnam Road, became the recruiting agent in the Cwmbran area by rejoining the South Wales Borderers in August 1914. The recruiting became very brisk by this time, and he enlisted a number of likely young men. Regularly would he be seen on the platform of the Cwmbran railway station, where he would give tremendous support to recruits who were leaving for the various depots. The mood of the people quickly changed from cheerful optimism to the grim acceptance of large casualty lists on the battlefields. John Fielding junior joined the Dorsetshire Regiment and survived, but his father soon learned that his eldest son Tom, serving with the South Wales Borderers, was killed on September 26th, 1914, during the retreat from Mons.

By the beginning of 1915, John Williams would be found on duty at the Brecon Depot. He was on the spot for the 6th annual dinner in commemoration of the 36th anniversary of the famous stand made by the 24th Regiment, and became a feature of the proceedings by being the only remaining Victoria Cross holder, of Rorke's Drift fame, present at the dinner. Held in the gymnasium decorated with a profusion of flags and bunting, the Union Jack and the green and white of the old regimental colours of the noble 24th, together with the portraits of Bromhead and Chard overlooking the proceedings. All of this made a grand setting for the evening. Perhaps, due to his recent great personal losses, his comrades that evening made a more than usual attempt to raise his spirits, for the health of Private Williams was enthusiastically received and he made a characteristic speech in return. On Sunday morning there was a parade of the veterans to the Priory Church, with the band heading the procession. Archdeacon Bevan preached to the large congregation. It was at the Brecon Depot he was to spend the remainder of the war. Although, those in authority had the greatest difficulty keeping him there, because he wanted to go "with the boys to the more active area and somewhere in France."

Like other parts of the country, Cwmbran experienced the hardships that a great war inflicts upon the civilian population. Pupils of St Dials Girls School would dispatch a regular consignment of knitted khaki woollen mittens to the Cwmbran men serving with the 2nd Mon. Regiment in France. A large collection of eggs given to the National Egg Collection Fund, for wounded and sick soldiers in hospital, would bring many interesting letters and postcards of appreciation to the young scholars, from as far away as France and Belgium.

The sad loss of young lives in Cwmbran and throughout the eastern valley of Monmouthshire was enormous, but there were also some war time stories that ended more fortunately. During the war, Mr William Scott, of Wesley Street, Cwmbran, had the proud distinction of having his six sons of military age serving with the Colours. His eldest son, Mr John Scott, joined the 1st Monmouthshires, whilst his other married son, Mr Joseph Scott, attached himself to the South Wales Borderers. Messrs Fred and Bramwell Scott both enlisted in the 5th Battalion, South Wales Borderers, and William Scott, junior, a playing member of the Cwmbran Cricket Club, joined the R.A.M.C. The youngest son, Thomas, belonged to the 2nd Monmouthshires. Amazingly, all of these young men were to survive the terrible slaughter. One of their six sisters, Elizabeth Scott, would tell of the village postman on his rounds with a dreaded telegram regularly visible in his hands. All the sisters would hold their breath each morning as he approached

John Henry Williams and John Williams

their house, hoping that he would not stop with the dreadful news of the loss of one of their brothers. Mercifully, he never stopped at their home, but, as the youngest sister recently remarked, "if it wasn't our house receiving the dreadful news it was sadly some other in Cwmbran."

In a conflict as large as a world war and lasting over a long period, it could only be expected that further heroes would emerge, as there were many more opportunities for brave acts to spontaneously take place. So it was, and quite rightly, the number of men who would wear the coveted cross, rose accordingly. A young man from Cwm, near Ebbw Vale, and also named John Williams, won the highest award and become a great friend of the Cwmbran V.C. holder. At Villers Outreaux, he went forward under heavy fire to the flank of the enemy post and rushed it single handed, capturing fifteen enemy soldiers. The prisoners soon realised that he was unaccompanied, and attempted to overpower him. He bayoneted five of them and the others quickly surrendered. Company Sergeant Major John Henry Williams, amazingly won at different times throughout the war the V.C., D.C.M., M.M. & Bar, and the Croix de Guerre. When receiving his awards, it was the first time the King had decorated the same man four times on the same day.

Those soldiers and sailors who were fortunate to return to the grateful village of Cwmbran, were feted with a meat tea and several smoking concerts. On the first Armistice day, at the Cwmbran Colliery, a number of men and boys assembled and observed the "King's two minutes." Mr F. Harris spoke a few kind words respecting the "boys" who had made the supreme sacrifice, and then Mr E. Thomas commenced the singing of the National Anthem, which was taken up and rendered most impressively by all present. It was indeed a very solemn two minutes.

At the time when reorganisation of the Brecon Depot was taking place, Sergeant John Williams demobilised as a private soldier in the recruiting office, on May 20th, 1920. A well attended benefit concert took place at the Brecon Barracks for the occasion and a varied and interesting programme carried out on a Wednesday evening raised the proceeds to the very satisfactory amount of around £33. He was by this time very well known and popular with the townspeople of Brecon who made a public presentation of a silver pocket watch. His send off from the Depot became a very enthusiastic event. Most of the army personnel turned out to send him on his way home and he was placed upon a gun carriage before being wheeled to the railway station. At the station, the Mayor of Brecon shook hands with the veteran, whose eyes filled with tears as the band played, and he once again bade farewell to the old 24th Foot. On his return to Cwmbran, he resumed his employment at the Nut and Bolt Works.

In the June of the same year, King George V and Queen Mary added a new small chapter to the history of the Victoria Cross by entertaining the recipients and their relatives at a garden party given in their honour.

Taken on the occasion of the Demobilisation of Pte. John Williams, V.C., 24th Regt., 26th May. 1920

BACK ROW: C.M.S.I. Edwards. C.Q.M.S. Wilcox, D.C.M Col. Sgt. Lewis. Sergt. Gibbs. Sergt. Barnes. Sergt. Sanders.
2nd ROW: Sgt. Drm. Sim. Ex-Sgt. Dr. Davies Sergt. Marsh. Sergt. Mason. C.S.M. Bleasdale. Sergt. Maher. Sergt. Lamont. Ex-Sergt. Rixon.
1st ROW: C.Q.M.S. Bowen. C.S.M. Barker, M.M. R.S.M. Bruntnell. Mr Atkins. Bt. Lt. Col. C.L. Taylor, D.S.O. Pte. J. Williams, V.C. R.Q.M.S. Woods, M.B.E. C.S.E. Wakefield. C.S.M. Matthews. Col. Sgt. Lloyd.

The King, with that kindly regard for his subjects which became so characteristic of him, so arranged the programme that before the garden party, the City of London had its opportunity of paying a tribute to the men who had won the coveted distinction of being classed as the bravest of the brave. John Fielding was amongst those who were entertained to luncheon by the officers of the Brigade of Guards at Wellington Barracks. Later, the holders of the Victoria Cross were marshalled into position for the walk to Buckingham Palace, via Birdcage Walk, the Horse Guards Parade, and the Mall.

Proceeded by the band of the Welsh Guards, and headed by a naval contingent, the little band of heroes passed between densely-crowded masses of people, who cheered them lustily, until they passed inside the gates of Buckingham Palace. Once inside, and in quieter surroundings, many of them heaved a sigh of relief. Most of the heroes were shy men, and to many of them, the march through the city was an ordeal with which they would have willingly gone without. Many of them carried the bronze cross in their pockets until the moment arrived when it had to be produced, and it went back in the pocket again at the earliest opportunity.

The garden of Buckingham Palace, with its fine spacious lawn and fringe of trees, hiding almost completely all signs of the London so close at hand, already contained the relatives. Between them and the terrace, the holders of the Victoria Cross were re-formed in order of seniority of award, and this having been done, the King and the Queen, accompanied by other members of the royal family, took their places on the terrace with a number of distinguished senior naval and military officers behind them.

The King, in the service uniform of a Field Marshal, and accompanied by the Duke of Connaught, and the young Princess Mary, first inspected the thin line of heroes drawn up on the lawn, before returning to the terrace steps where each of the heroes was to be presented individually.

As each man approached the King, his name was announced together with the name of the campaign or theatre of war in which he won his cross. The King and Queen shook hands with each man as he passed, and said a few words to them. After the few remaining veterans of the Indian Mutiny, and another who won his cross in China in 1860, came Private John Williams, whose name conjured up memories of the gallant defence of the hospital at Rorke's Drift. Three hundred and ten brave men were to meet their Sovereign on this unique occasion.

After the presentations had all been made, refreshments were served, and many of the guests formed small parties on the lawn. Later, the members of the Royal Family moved among them, with a lack of formality which surprised some of the visitors. The younger V.C.s busily engaged themselves in collecting the autographs of their seniors, to be kept in memory of a wonderful afternoon.(33)

Desiring a club of their own, the Cwmbran Comrades of the Great War had, for the last few years, worked most diligently to achieve this goal. Organised sports events and concerts brought in some of the necessary funds, whilst assistance by local firms and well-known people in the district, soon brought the completion of the venture within their reach. One of the early objectives of the club was to keep the Comrades together and arrange sports and games for the young and old. Messrs Guest, Keen, and Nettlefold had very kindly let them have about eight and a half acres of land for this purpose, and an old army hut of corrugated iron was erected alongside Coronation Road, about three minutes walk from the Cwmbran G.W.R. Railway Station. The hut was only intended to be used as a temporary measure until funds could be raised to build a more permeant structure. The Cwmbran Comrades Club of the Great War and Institute, which also inclued Llantarnam, unofficially opened in June of 1921, and a rugby football team soon formed and played in the field adjoining the Institute. Armistice Day became the natural choice for the official opening and at this time there was a membership of 317, out of which 283 were ex-service men.

For the official opening, the premises were gaily decorated with patriotic flags. Colonel T.W. Pearson, D.S.O., of the Royal Artillery, and former highly esteemed Welsh International rugby three-quarter, who actually captained the national fifteen, became the clubs first president, with Mr John Hardy as chairman. Mr L. Forester-Walker, M.P., performed the official opening and among the many present was Mr John Williams V.C., a tremendous supporter of the venture, who had recently been presented to H.R.H. the Prince of Wales, on the occasion of his visit to Newport.

In October 1921, Mrs Margaret Fielding, aged 82 years, died, and was buried in the Cwmbran cemetery.

Also in December of the same year, the Cwmbran Territorials came into possession of their own Drill Hall. The detachment had hitherto been quartered in the Council Offices, but an old army hut was intended to serve admirably until such time as a hall of bricks and mortar could be forthcoming. Among those who strived hard to make this possible was Lieutenant Owen, Company Quarter-Master Love, D.C.M., Sergeant-Major Thomas, a champion cross country runner, and Mr John Williams, V.C.

In 1922, John Fielding, aged 65 years, retired from his occupation in the Nut and Bolt Section of the Guest, Keen, and Nettlefolds Works at Cwmbran. Here he had spent most of his civilian working life except for a short time as a schoolteacher at the St. Patrick's Boys' School, Middlesborough. Although remembered by the pupils as a kindly, unassuming man, he did not enjoy the life as an academic and returned to South Wales. Prior to retirement, he is known to have been an operator of a nut cutting machine at the works. The nuts and bolts produced were mainly for the railway industry and would be sent all over the world. Just prior to his retirement, he instructed a young man by the name of Frank H. Johnston, a former Welsh half mile champion and Powderhall sprinter, in the operating procedure of his cutting machine. It was the son of this well known athlete who later married one of Mr Fielding's granddaughters.

Although sixty-five years of age, nothing would have prevented the Cwmbran man from attending the memorial ceremony to the South Wales Borderers held at Brecon towards the end of May, 1922. The impressive ceremony was performed in St. John's (Priory) Church, on a Thursday. For the solemn occasion, the Havard Chapel had been restored and adorned by the regiment in memory of the 5,777 officers and men of the various battalions of the South Wales Borderers who fell in the Great War. The Bishop of Swansea delivered the dedication, and a tablet recording the fact was unveiled by the Colonel of the Regiment, Lieutenant-General Sir A.S. Cobbe, V.C. A striking figure in the spectacular parade proved to be Private John Williams, V.C., the sole survivor of the South Wales Borderers Victoria Cross heroes of Rorke's Drift. To be seen in his white gloved hands, and carried with the greatest care and dignity, was the roll of honour. The handsome book contained the names of so many brave men, including his eldest son, Tom.

John Fielding settled well into retirement, although existing on a meagre pension became very difficult for anyone in those bygone days. He continued to partake of his one pint of beer each evening and enjoyed giving great support to the Cwmbran Comrades Institute by becoming a regular presenter of prizes for various sporting activities. When football medals were handed out by the veteran hero, he would enthusiastically exhort the receivers to aim for greater things on the playing fields. The flourishing Territorial Unit also kept the hero very busy. At the annual Xmas prize presentation and supper of 'A' company, he would be asked to present prizes for musketry. In 1925, the honorary members of the Company took advantage of the occasion to present Captain R.D. Owen with a suitable inscribed impressive sword. Mr. Fielding made the presentation and described the recipient as an open-minded and worthily popular officer, who always treated his men with the utmost kindness. Captain Owen suitable responded and explained that much of the success of 'A' Company was due to the active interest taken in the members by ex-Private John Williams, whose footsteps he had endeavoured to follow.

Tremendous excitement prevailed in the Eastern Valley of Monmouthshire in the beginning of August 1924. Hard work and careful planning set the scene for a highly successful Royal Welsh National Eisteddfod at Pontypool. Held in the picturesque Pontypool Park, one of the many highlights of the week was the visit by H.R.H. the Prince of Wales. Arriving at the Pontypool Road Station, which was bedecked with flags and emblems, the popular Prince unexpectedly asked to make an unscheduled stop at the nearby Panteg memorial to those who died in the Great War, for the purpose of laying a wreath. A large gathering of people eagerly awaited his arrival in the park. After receiving an enormous welcome, he proceeded to tour the arena and showed great interest in all he saw. On the sides of the large exhibition ring were 1,120 ex-Servicemen forming a huge square and prepared for inspection. On nearing the ex-Servicemen's guard of honour, he raised his hat to Mr Roderick's band in passing. The Prince commenced his own inspection and was most concerned in his enquiries to those who had lost a limb. After speaking to Mr William Cooper, Chairman of the Panteg British Legion, he stopped in front of Mr John Williams, of Cwmbran, and on whose jacket he could see the most famous of medals. On the invitation of the Prince, the Cwmbran man took one pace forward and had his hand shaken most heartily by the heir to the throne. The Prince chatted pleasantly to Mr Williams for a while and was pleased to learn that his brother, Mr Dennis Fielding, a veteran of many campaigns, was standing nearby. The photographs of this memorable few moments not only appeared in the local newspapers, but also the national press.

On November 11th, 1924, every one in Pontnewydd, the small village alongside Cwmbran, at last witnessed the long awaited memorial to those in the district who had died in the Great War. The memorial in the form of an obelisk was unveiled by the veteran Lord Treowen. John Williams V.C., stood in front of the memorial during the deeply felt ceremony. Afterwards he chatted to his Lordship, who upon learning the age of the Cwmbran man surprisingly remarked: "You are an older soldier than I am!"

On the occasion of his 67th birthday, the members of the Cwmbran branch of the British Legion honoured the local man and hung his inscribed portrait in their headquarters. John Williams, V.C., of immortal Rorke's Drift fame, who on numerous occasions had been honoured since the memorable stand on January 22nd, 1879, was again lionised the following year at a smoking concert held at the Drill Hall, where he became the recipient of a most suitable gift.

As naturally expected, the veteran hero, in his sixty-eighth year, had become a most familiar figure at many functions, and in order that he might appear on special occasions suitably dressed, the officers, warrant officers, sergeants, and

The Prince shakes hands with Mr. John Williams, V.C., with whom he chatted.

honorary members of the Sports Club and Institute connected with the 2nd Monmouthshire Drill Hall, presented him with a smart suit of blue patrol with the badge of his old regiment.

Lieutenant W.A.C. Matthews who commanded 'A' Company remarked in his long speech that Sergeant Williams had for many years been the means of keeping the Company at Cwmbran up to strength. He also added that he was the only man outside the regiment and the immediate past members, who had been allowed to wear the smart undress uniform in which they saw him that evening.

Sergeant John Williams replied by saying it was a pleasure to be among the officers, warrant officers, and comrades. After thanking all for the gift, he remarked, "If I was a younger man I would be in the colours now."

Captain C.H. Morgan, of the South Wales Borderers, and adjutant of the Battalion, complimented Sergeant Williams publicly upon his smart appearance, and declared that if they all looked as neat as Sergeant Williams did that night, when they had almost reached the allotted span, they would do well. He exhorted the younger men present to take Sergeant Williams for a pattern worthy of emulation and could not help thinking what a splendid example he was to them all.

At sixty-eight years of age, the veteran was at this time found to be remarkably alert, and as a life member of the Mess and Sports Club and Institute of the Cwmbran Company, of the 2nd Battalion Monmouthshire Regiment, he still took an absorbing interest in the institution amongst which members he remained extremely popular. During the concert that followed, the usually reticent hero heartily joined in the proceedings, one of his contributions being "The Dear Little Shamrock," the chorus of which went with a rollicking swing.(34)

With a daffodil as a buttonhole, a stirring welcome announced the arrival of the Prince of Wales at the Cardiff rugby ground, prior to the International match between Wales and Scotland on Saturday, February 5th, 1927. In the crowd for that memorable game was John Fielding, a passionate Welsh rugby supporter. He enjoyed the game before leaving for the United Services' Club where he was a life member of the mess. He, with five others, who were Sergt.-Major John Henry Williams, V.C., (South Wales Borders), Lieut. J. Grimshaw, V.C., (of the Lancashire Fusiliers, and chief recruiting officer for South Wales), Captain E. Beachcroft Beckwith Towse, V.C., (the blind hero of the Gordon Highlanders), Sergeant Sam Vickery, V.C., (of the Dorsetshire Regiment) and Private H.W. Lewis, V.C., who hailed from Milford Haven, were introduced to the Prince of Wales. As he shook hands with the veterans, all felt the warmness of his greeting, the freedom of his manner, and the easiness of his conversation. It was his understanding of human nature which struck them most, for it was not the bloody fields of battle on which they had so distinguished themselves that he asked, but of their present position and health.

"Hello," he said to the veteran of Rorke's Drift, "where did we meet last? Was it at Pontypool?" "Yes sir," replied John Williams, of Cwmbran, "and here - the last time you came to the International." The only setback on what would have been a perfect day for the old campaigner was the result of the International match, which went Scotland's way by five points to nil.

1929 was to be a busy year for John Williams. As well as his local engagements, this became a special year with the 50th anniversary of Rorke's Drift about to be commemorated. It had been the custom of the 2nd Battalion of the South Wales Borderers to celebrate the brave defence of Rorke's Drift on the 22nd of January, but that year it fell awkwardly, for the battalion was at Aden under orders for home. Due to these circumstances it was decided to hold the celebrations on March 31st and April 1st, and the re-union would involve the long trek to Portsmouth for many of the old campaigners.

On Saturday November 9th, of the same year, John Williams experienced a more exciting and a more demanding engagement. He was to be among the 321 Victoria Cross holders brought together to attend a dinner organised by the British Legion in the Royal Gallery of the House of Lords. Two reasons explained why this unique reunion attracted a so remarkable company to London. One was to be associated with a united appeal to the nation for help for ex-Service men who were in need, and for the widows and dependants of those who gave their lives in the Great War. The other gave the rare opportunity to be among the guests who would meet the Prince of Wales.

The V.C.s who attended, were from all parts of the Empire, and included the two remaining Rorke's Drift survivors, those from the Afghan and Burma campaigns, the two wars with the Boers, and other fights of a period before war on a world wide scale had been considered possible. Lieutenant Colonel J.H. Reynolds and John Williams were the two senior holders of the award, as the three veterans of the Indian Mutiny, who were present at the Royal Garden Party in 1920, had since had the "Last Post" sounded for them.

A large crowd gathered outside the Houses of Parliament to see the arrival of the V.C.s, and the guests, who were obviously embarrassed by the cheering warmth of their reception, hurried along a lane kept with difficulty through the crowd. Early arrivals had a long wait before the reception by their Royal host began. These wandered around the Peers lobby and gradually began to enter into conversation. Each V.C. wore on the opposite coat lapel to his medals, a blue disc giving his name and unit. By half past seven the company, then on comfortable terms with each other, had spread into the House of Lords, and then the unique spectacle could be seen of scores of men, without a thought of politics, using the red benches of the Upper Chamber as a lounge.

Eventually, the reception by the Prince, who, like every one else present, wore a lounge suit, began, and the V.C.s slowly filed through the elegant Princes' Chamber to shake hands with him and pass on to their place at the table in the Royal Gallery. The Prince immediately recognised the Cwmbran man and greeted him with "Hullo, Williams!" They chatted for a short time, and as Private Williams told a reporter afterwards, they just "had a few words about old times."

Military rank and social standing counted for nothing at this unprecedented and astonishing dinner. Seats had been allocated by the drawing of numbers and

---

Toasts

"The King"
H.R.H. THE PRINCE OF WALES, K.G.

"The Royal Family"
ADMIRAL OF THE FLEET EARL JELLICOE,
G.C.B., O.M.

"The Guests"
H.R.H. THE PRINCE OF WALES

Responses will be made on behalf of Navy, Army,
Air Force and Overseas V.C.'s respectively by
LIEUT.-COMMANDER H. AUTEN, V.C., D.S.O.
SERGEANT C. E. SPACKMAN, V.C.
LIEUT.-COLONEL W. A. BISHOP, V.C.,
D.S.O., M.C., D.F.C.
and
LIEUT.-COLONEL G. R. PEARKES, V.C.,
D.S.O., M.C.

the Prince of Wales as chairman had a chauffeur sitting on his right side. Flanders poppies dominated the setting for the dinner. When John Williams arrived at his place at the table, he found a pleasant surprise awaiting him. His chair appeared different from all others. It was a plain wooden chair which had been taken from the hospital at Rorke's Drift. Rumour has it that the elderly veteran, renowned for his dry sense of humour, thoroughly enjoyed the gesture. Alongside him at the table were Captain C.H. Frisby, V.C., Coldstream Guards, and Lieutenant W.A. White, V.C., M.G. Corps, who both won their medals during the last year of the Great War. There was very little talk of military matters at the table and the conversation in the main was mostly about football, with some explaining how they would have scored the all important goal that Saturday afternoon.

Speeches when they came, were short and soon over. In his address, the Prince of Wales described the "most enviable Order of the Victoria Cross" as "the most democratic and at the same time the most exclusive of all orders of chivalry." During the last half hour, the gathering sang "Tommy songs" as these were played by the band of the Grenadier Guards. The Prince of Wales industriously signed programmes of the many who sought his name to increase the interest of a well designed souvenir of the night.

On the following Monday, November 11th, around 300 of the Victoria Cross holders took part in the eleventh anniversary of the signing of the Armistice, at the Cenotaph in Whitehall. In the rain, and in columns of four, they led the procession of ex-Service men and women to the Cenotaph and were the first to salute the

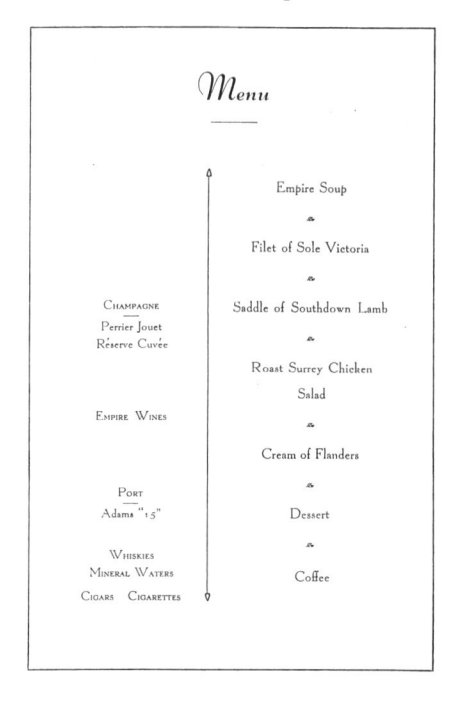

Menu

Empire Soup

Filet of Sole Victoria

CHAMPAGNE
Perrier Jouet
Réserve Cuvée

Saddle of Southdown Lamb

Roast Surrey Chicken
Salad

EMPIRE WINES

Cream of Flanders

PORT
Adams "15"

Dessert

WHISKIES
MINERAL WATERS
CIGARS   CIGARETTES

Coffee

Edward

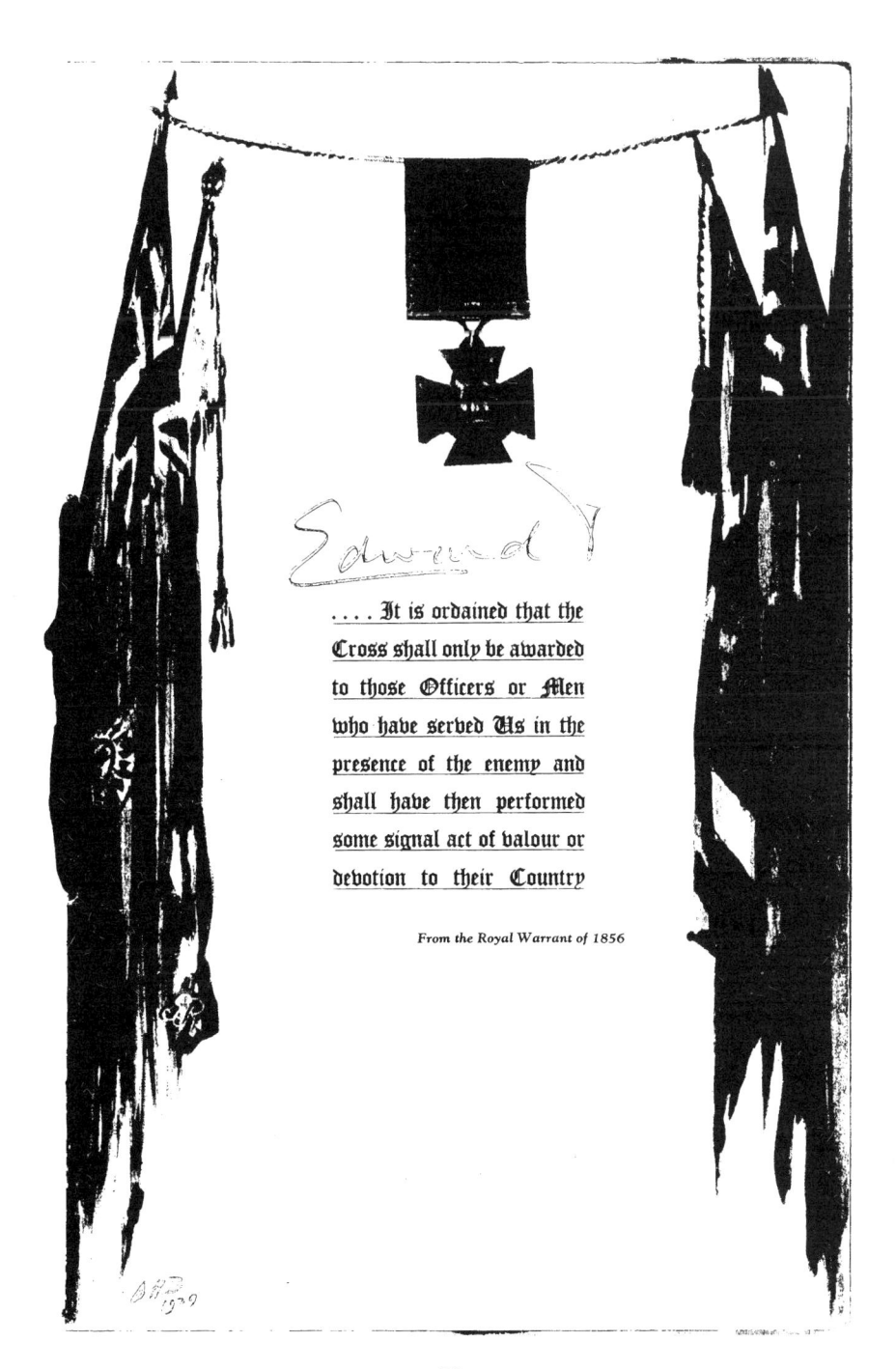

.... It is ordained that the Cross shall only be awarded to those Officers or Men who have served Us in the presence of the enemy and shall have then performed some signal act of valour or devotion to their Country

From the Royal Warrant of 1856

nation's monument to the fallen after the short service of commemoration had ended.

At a special concert at the Albert Hall in the evening, the V.C.s were cheered enthusiastically as they took their seats, but one is known to have been absent from this last pleasant duty. Though he had enjoyed himself at the V.C.s dinner, and took part in the march to the Cenotaph, the excitement had been too much for the seventy two year old John Williams, and he returned home early.(35)

To those in Cwmbran it was thought that he was returning on Tuesday, and the branch of the British Legion made elaborate plans to give him a warm "welcome home." The Cwmbran Brass Band was to have met him at the railway station and escort him to the British Legion Club, where a great celebration had been planned. Consequently, it was a great shock to the organisers of the reception to learn that their hero had returned quite unostentatiously on Monday night. He had been greeted by nothing more than the "Tickets, please" of the station porter. The following day, he was resting in bed, when the train thought to contain him, pulled into the Cwmbran station.(36)

The sun shone brightly on that particular summer day, as John Fielding stood, with his walking stick in hand, on the pavement alongside the narrow valley road. On each side of him were to be seen expectant onlookers in summer clothes. Grandmothers were waiting with young children skipping around their skirts, as

---

Programme of Music
BY
The String Band of H.M. Grenadier Guards
BY PERMISSION OF COLONEL LORD HENRY C. SEYMOUR, D.S.O.

1. March — — "Martial Moments" — — arr. *Winter*
2. Overture — "The Return from Abroad" — *Mendelssohn*
3. Valse from — "The Student Prince" — — — *Romberg*
4. Selection — "The New Moon" — — — *Romberg*
5. Two Fox-Trots (a) "Wedding of the Painted Doll" } *Brown*
   (b) "Broadway Melody" — —
6. Grand Selection — — "Faust" — — — *Gounod*
7. Three Dale Dances — — — — — — — *Wood*
8. Excerpts from — "Hold Everything" — *Henderson*
9. Songs 1914 to 1918 "Tommies' Tunes" — arr. *Stoddon*
10. Quick-Step — — "A Bunch of Roses" — — *Chapi*

Director of Music:
CAPTAIN G. MILLER, P.S.M., L.R.A.M.

80

their mothers did a generation before. The excitement increased as the carnival procession drew near. Each colourful exhibit on the back of the large lorries was greeted with a cheer and the clapping of young hands as it passed by. Coming nearer, an exhibit was meeting with loud approval. The howls of laughter, the boos of derision, and the uncomplimentary remarks made one wonder what was about to be witnessed. As the exhibit drew alongside the elderly man, the good natured smile froze on his face and disappeared. He turned on his heels and slowly began to walk home, his afternoon completely spoiled. The exhibit, portraying a scene from the Zulu War, moved along with the bodies covered in black shoe polish cavorting on the precarious platform. As the old man drew nearer home he thought of the Zulu warriors, whose discipline many European armies would have envied. He remembered their bravery, when time and again they ran at the withering fire from the British guns. The hell experienced by both sides in that life or death struggle, all those years before, had nurtured a worthy respect on each side for the courage of their opponents. On arriving home, his daughter learned of his obvious distress in a few angry, faltering sentences. The young people taking part in the parade would not have understood the thoughts of this elderly man, whose mind conjured up pictures of nearly half a century before. Through his eyes, the grotesque, though unintentional disrespectful scene just witnessed, had become a sign of his own physical mortality.

| Major | Captain | Colonel | Colonel | Captain |
| L. A. Mitchell. | J. H. E. Webb. | W. R. Lewis, T.D | W. D. S. Brownrigg. | J. S. Windsor, M.C. |

Sgt. John Williams V.C.

82

Chapter Seven

LAST POST

The survivors of the Zulu War campaign of 1879 were few and rapidly becoming fewer by 1931. "Soon we will all be gone," remarked one of the veterans. On February 20th, 1931, the Free Press of Monmouthshire had the sad task of reporting the death of one of the few remaining survivors of the epic struggle at Rorke's Drift. Mr William Osborne, of 79 Cambrian Row, Blaenavon, had died on the morning before, aged 73 years. He had been born in Duke Street, Blaenavon, the son of Thomas Osborne, who was employed for many years at the Blaenavon Company Mills. On completion of six years regular service, he returned from India to Blaenavon in 1883 at the age of 26 years. It was here he began to work underground for the Blaenavon Company and married Miss Martha Whitcombe, daughter of Mr and Mrs Joseph Whitcombe, of Abersychan.

The funeral became fully military, with the coffin borne from the house at Cambrian Row to St. Peter's Churchyard on a gun carriage, which had been brought from Newport, and was drawn by six horses. Included among the many mourners were two other defenders of Rorke's Drift, Private J.S. Jobbins, Pontnewynydd, and Private John Williams, V.C., of Cwmbran.

Just over a year later, on March 4th, 1932, Doctor James Reynolds, V.C., died peacefully in a London nursing home. This sad event left John Fielding as the only one remaining alive of the eleven recipients who won the Victoria Cross at Rorke's Drift.

John Fielding had reached the age of 75 years, and by this time neighbours were well used to the large saloon motorcar, with army escort, arriving outside the house to take the elderly gentleman away to various military functions. No doubt saddened by the loss of so many friends and comrades, he still attempted to remain cheerful whilst in the company of those he loved. When the day came around to collect his pension, his daughters would regularly be asked which grandchildren were due for new shoes, a priority so necessary in his younger days. Although possessing a heart that was slowly failing, he would still enjoy his usual walk from 28, Cocker Avenue, Cwmbran, where he had been living for some time with his daughter, Mrs Margaret Pratley, to the home of another daughter, Mrs Elizabeth Catherine Jones, of 7, Tycoch, Cwmbran. Here he would enjoy his regular cup of

Bovril and a pipe of tobacco, whilst being kept up to date with family events before returning home.

On November 24th, 1932, John Fielding experienced his favourite walk along the quiet towpath of the Monmouthshire Canal for the last time. The great man arrived at the Tycoch home of his daughter in a distressed state and obviously very ill. Mrs Jones gentle laid her ailing father on a couch and his physician, Dr. F. Carlton Jones M.B., was immediately summoned. Everything that could be done to make the old soldier comfortable became the first priority. Sadly, nothing could reverse the myocardial degeneration of his heart and the old warrior passed away at five o'clock the following Friday morning.

The Times newspaper announced the death of the famous Cwmbran inhabitant to the world the following day, and the issue included a lengthy memoir.

Arrangements for the funeral to take place on Tuesday, November 29th, fell to Mr Arthur A. Simmonds, a Cwmbran undertaker, and the place of burial was to be in the churchyard of the venerated church of Saint Michael of All Angels, Llantarnam. This ancient church stood alongside what was then the main road leading into Cwmbran, from the direction of the large town of Newport. Although regarded as an appropriated church of the nearby Llantarnam Abbey, it is suggested that a celtic church was present on the site long before the Abbey came into existence. Today, a modern road by-passes the church which for a brief moment in time, in that bygone year, became known all over the world.

Prior to the funeral, there was a lying-in-state overnight in Our Lady of the Angels Church, Wesley Street, Cwmbran. Some still remember the four hourly changing of the guard of honour during that long night. The vigilant guard were C.Q.M.S. Kelly, Sergeants S. Coleman, P. Reynolds, H. Love, and Lance-Sergeants A. Davies and G. Powell, of "A" (M.G.) Company.

On Tuesday, November 29th, 1932, hundreds travelled to Cwmbran, either on foot along the towpath of the Monmouthshire Canal, or by public transport, to pay their last respects to a man who had become a legend in the fullest meaning of the word. In his life he had been humble and yet he was known to a great Queen and several Kings of Great Britain. He could be equally at ease talking to the ruling classes of the land as he could be when chatting to the man who would sweep the floor at the Cwmbran Nut and Bolt Works. His greatness lay in the fact that not only had he bravely won on his own merit, the highest award for courage, but that he also earned the award a second time by respecting the honour surrounding the Victoria Cross, and becoming a valued representative of the British Army.

Canon J. Jarvis, Cwmbran's Catholic priest, celebrated the Mass and performed the last rites at the Catholic Church, Wesley Street, and the procession re-formed for the march to the Llantarnam Churchyard.

Immediately in front of the gun carriage could be observed the guard of honour and band and drums of the 2nd Battalion Monmouthshire Regiment, under bandmaster T. Valentine. They were to play the "Dead March in Saul" en route. The coffin, covered by the Union Jack, was borne on a gun carriage, which, together with a team of six magnificent horses, was provided by the 2nd Brigade R.H.A., Newport Barracks. Behind the gun carriage, Regimental Sergeant Major Theobald carried, on a velvet cushion, the Victoria Cross and other medals of the gallant soldier.

Conveyed in motorcars, the chief mourners were Messrs William Fielding and John Fielding, Port Talbot, sons; Mrs Margaret Pratley, Mr and Mrs E. Catherine

Jones, Cwmbran, son-in law and daughters; Messrs Maurice, Joseph and Dennis Fielding (Pontnewydd), William and Michael Fielding, Port Talbot, brothers; and W. Abbot, a cousin from Liverpool.

A place of honour in the procession, which extended over a half a mile, was given to the survivors of the Zulu War of 1879. These were Messrs William Prosser, Nantyglo; Phillip Price, Blaina; George Purnell, Pontypool; John Powell, Abergavenny; John Jobbins, Pontnewynydd; and Charles Jones, Pontypool.

These elderly gentlemen were followed by the British Legion Standard bearers who were: Messrs D. Davies, Cwmbran; William Lloyd, Panteg; H. Merrick, Ebbw Vale; C. James, Newport; S. Cotterell, Pontypool; F. Harvey, D.C.M., Pontnewynydd; and W.J. Beynon, County standard bearer.

The pall-bearers were Sergeants F. Bromley, C. Rice, R. Weaver, J. Alders, E. Morris, I. Rawlinson, W. Price, and W. Lowray, of the Brecon Depot, S.W.B. The Regiment was represented by Lieutenant-Colonel A. Ellis Williams, D.S.O., M.C., Commanding the Depot, Brecon; Lieutenant-Colonel Gwynne C. Thomas, D.S.O., O.B.E., Newport, Secretary 24th Regimental Association; Captain T.P. Robertson, Captain J.S. Winsor, M.C. (Adjutant 2nd Monmouths). Lieutenants F.F.S. Barlow, G.B. Sugden, and J. McGuire.

Behind the firing party and bearers followed a strong detachment of Panteg Battery of the 83rd Brigade R.A. (T.), under Major Walter E. Grey, T.D. Next came a representative contingent of the 2nd Monmouths under Captain J.H.E. Webb and Captain W.A.C. Matthews and R.S.M. H. Hartigan, O.B.E., and a party of N.C.O.'s of the 1st (Rifle) Battalion Monmouthshire Regiment, under C.S.M. Reg Chick, M.C.

There was also a strong representation of the Cwmbran branch of the Legion, led by Lieutenant J.A. Burgoyne (President), ex-C.S.M. J.H. Williams, V.C., D.C.M., M.M., of the South Wales Borderers, Ebbw Vale, and Mr. W.J. Smith, D.S.M., Chairman of the County Committee of the British Legion, led about five hundred members who represented every branch in the county.

Among old comrades of the Regiment and others present were Major E.K. Lanman, D.S.O., M.C., Dinas Powis; Major H.C. Pauncefort-Munday, O.B.E., Newport; Captain J.C. Owen, M.C., Pontypridd; Lieutenant R.I. Fairfax, M.C., Cwmbran; ex-R.S.M.'s H.B. Andrews, Brecon; G. Steward, Abergavenny; J. Makepeace; ex-C.S.M. Ferrigan, Brecon; ex-Colour Sergeant H. Standen, D.C.M., C.Q.M.S. G. Gibbs, M.M., Chepstow; ex-C.S.M. C.E.W. Parrish, D.C.M., Newport; ex-Sergeant W.H. Thomas, Mr E.C. Capel, Newport, with representatives from all the Service battalions; Thomas Press (representing the City of London Branch of the British Legion); ex Sergeant Major Talmadge, Caerleon; Lt.-col. Christopher, Major J.D. Dunbar and Captain Fox (representing the Union Jack Club, Newport); and ex-Sergt-Major Andrews (Brecon Dept. S.W.B.); Messrs G.W. Elliott, chairman, H. Williams, treasurer, and H. Jones, secretary (representing the Pontnewydd British Legion); Messrs W. Crowley, chairman, J. Cohane, vice-president, R. Griffiths, secretary, and J. Hardy, treasurer (representing Cwmbran British Legion); Councillors A. McIlrath, J.P., F.C. Parkes and J. Griffin (Llanfrechfa U.D.C.); the Rev. John Donne, B.A., vicar of Llantarnam; Councillors Rowland Jarret; J. Daley, and A.H. Viney, surveyors (representing Llantarnam U.D.C.)

The Mayor of Brecon (Captain B. Francis) represented the town and marched with the ex-Service men.

All of Cwmbran turned out, with many hundreds lining the route, to pay a final tribute to its Victoria Cross hero. In every street through which the solemn procession passed, the blinds were drawn, and schools and business premises were closed during the time of the funeral. The streets were thronged with people who stood in silence with bowed heads as the cortege passed. A good number of newspaper reporters and camera men filled the crowd, and the Pathe News movie cameras recorded the unique event to show in cinemas all over the country and abroad.

The scene at Saint Michael's of All Angels Church would not be forgotten by those present on that sad day. The churchyard was almost full before the long procession entered. Some even climbed to the top of the church tower to gain a better view.

Canon Jarvis gave the committal rites. Three volleys were fired over the grave and buglers sounded the "Last Post" and "Reveille."

Hundreds passed around the grave in silence and inspected the floral tributes.

The floral tributes from the Regimental Association were in the form of a Maltese Cross, which forms the centre of the regimental cap badge.
Among the many and beautiful wreaths was one "To the last memory of 1395 Private John Williams, V.C., 'B' Company Second Battalion 24th Regiment, one of the defenders of Rorke's Drift, January 22nd and 23rd, 1879, from Charles Hitch, Darlington, County Durham.
Among others who sent flowers were:- Brigadier-General I.G. Morgan-Owen, Colonel, South Wales Borderers; Officers, N.C.O.'s and men "A" (M.G.) Company 2nd Monmouths; all ranks "B" Company 2nd Battalion of the S.W.B.; Officers, N.C.O.'s and men 2nd Battalion Monmouthshire Regiment; Brevet Colonel, Officers, Warrant Officers, N.C.O.'s and men of the 3rd Monmouths; Territorial Club, Cwmbran; South Wales Borderers Regimental Association "From the survivors of the defence of Rorke's Drift, Frank Bourne, Alfred Saxty, Thomas Buckley, Peter Cane, William Cooper, George Edwards, Henry Martin, John Jobbins, George Deacon, Calib Wood."

Other wreaths were: Union Jack Club, Newport; all ranks of the 1st (Rifle) Battalion Monmouthshire Regiment; Wales Area Council British Legion; Workingmen's Club and Institute, Cwmbran; Comrades of the Cwmbran branch of the Legion; British Legion, Abergavenny; Women's Section of the Cwmbran British Legion; United Services Mess, Cardiff; Pontnewydd branch of the Legion; Son and Grandson of the late Sergeant Hook, V.C., Rorke's Drift; Pontnewydd Workingmen's Club; Cwmbran Conservative Club; all ranks, Depot, South Wales Borderers; all ranks 1st Battalion South Wales Borderers; all ranks 2nd Battalion South Wales Borderers, with the inscription "In proud memory of John Williams, V.C."(37)

CWMBRAN, WALES.

Britain's oldest V.C.

Hail & farewell to
MR. JOHN FIELDING —
better known as
Private JOHN WILLIAMS V.C. —
hero of Rorke's drift in
1879 /

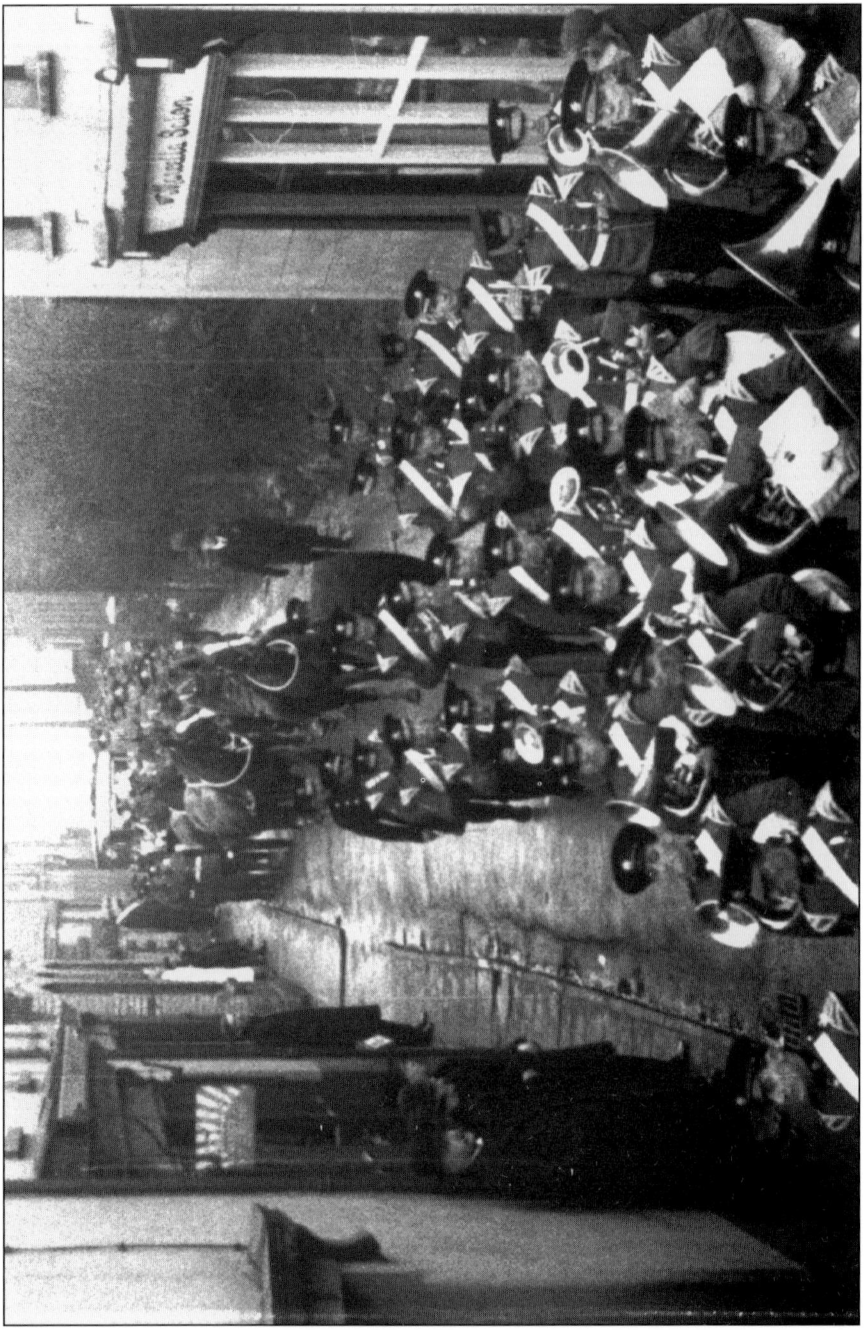

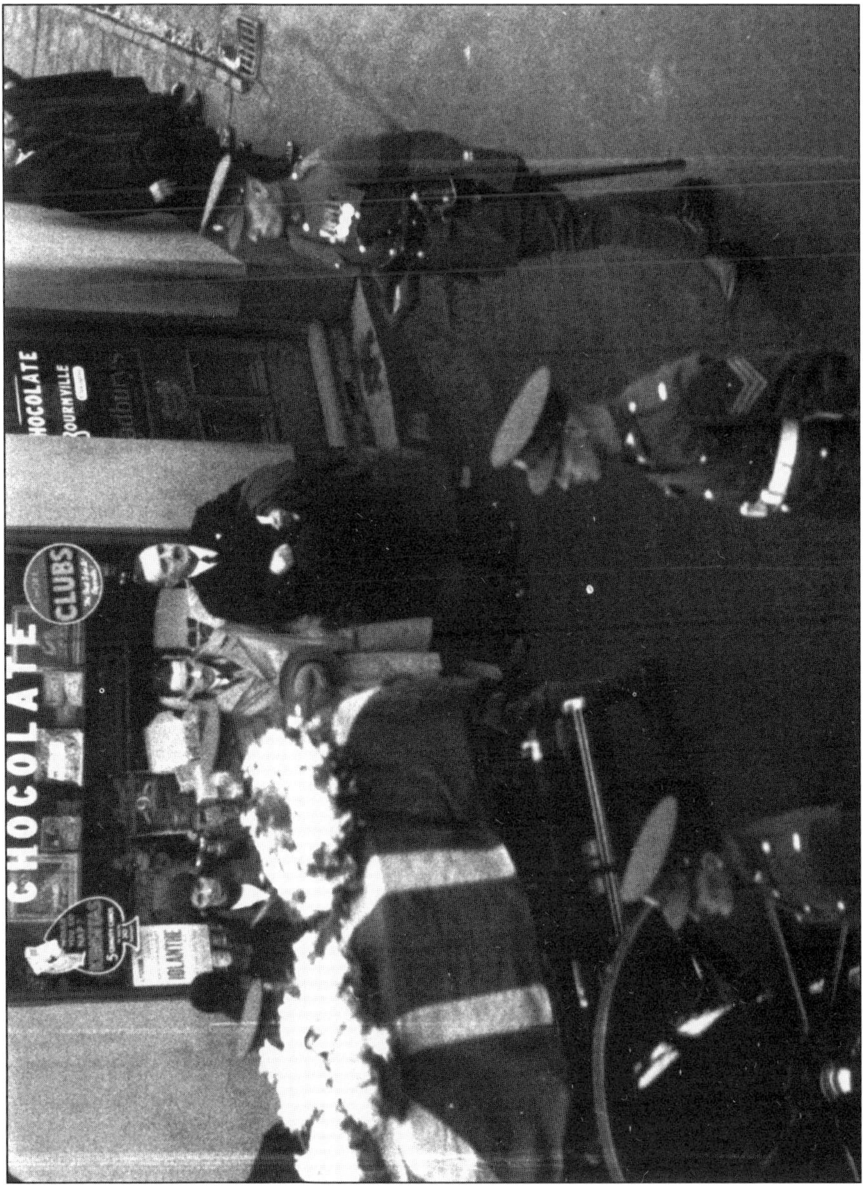
CHOCOLATE
CLUBS
CHOCOLATE
BOURNVILLE

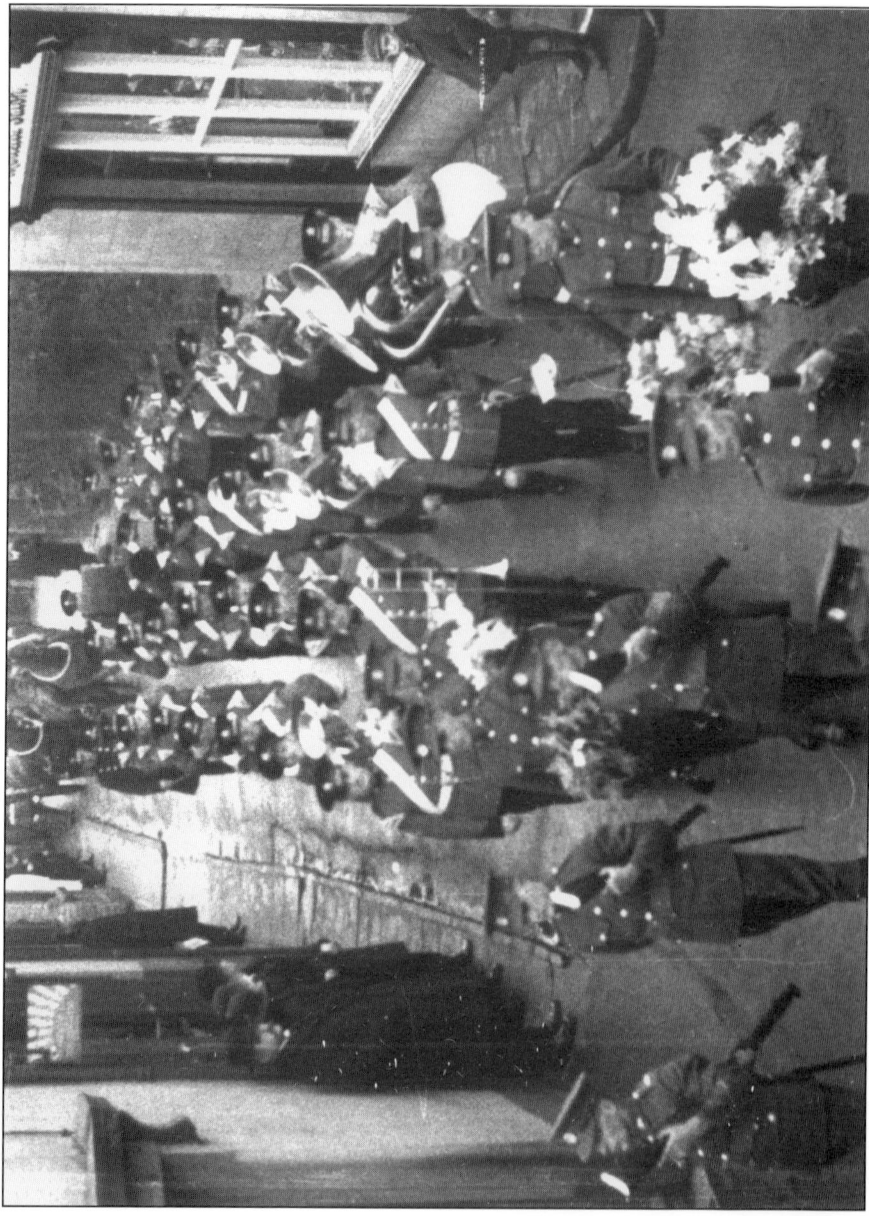

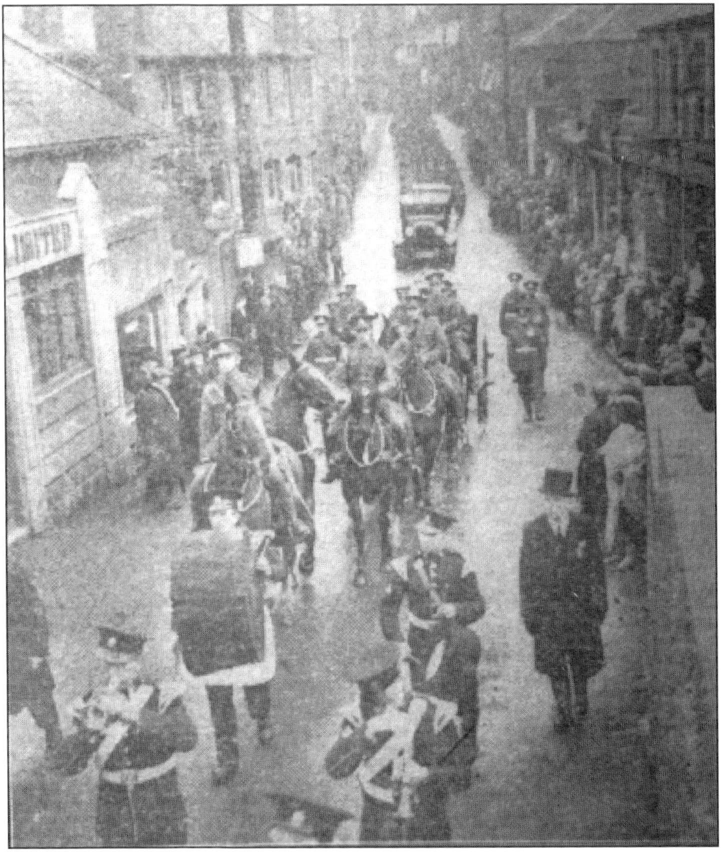

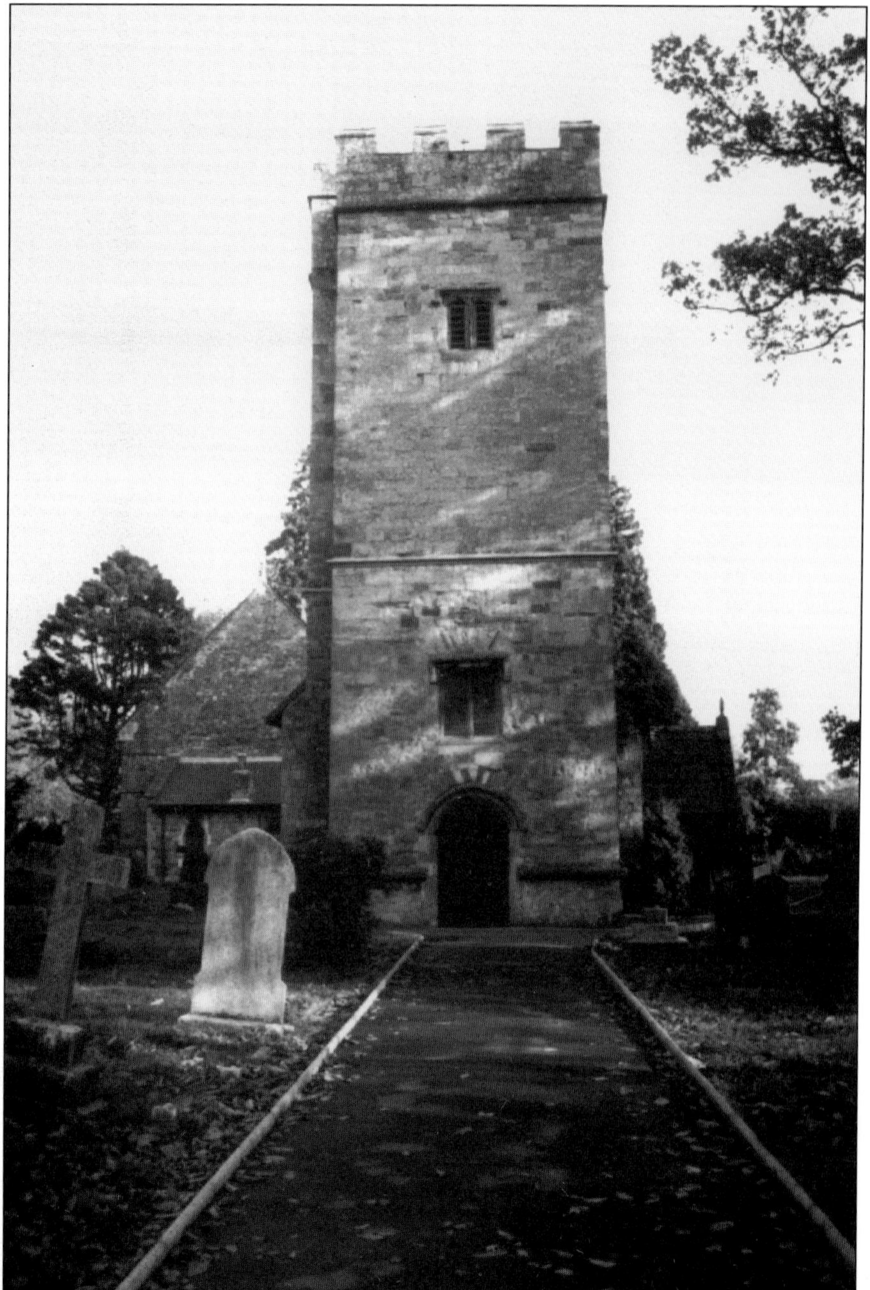

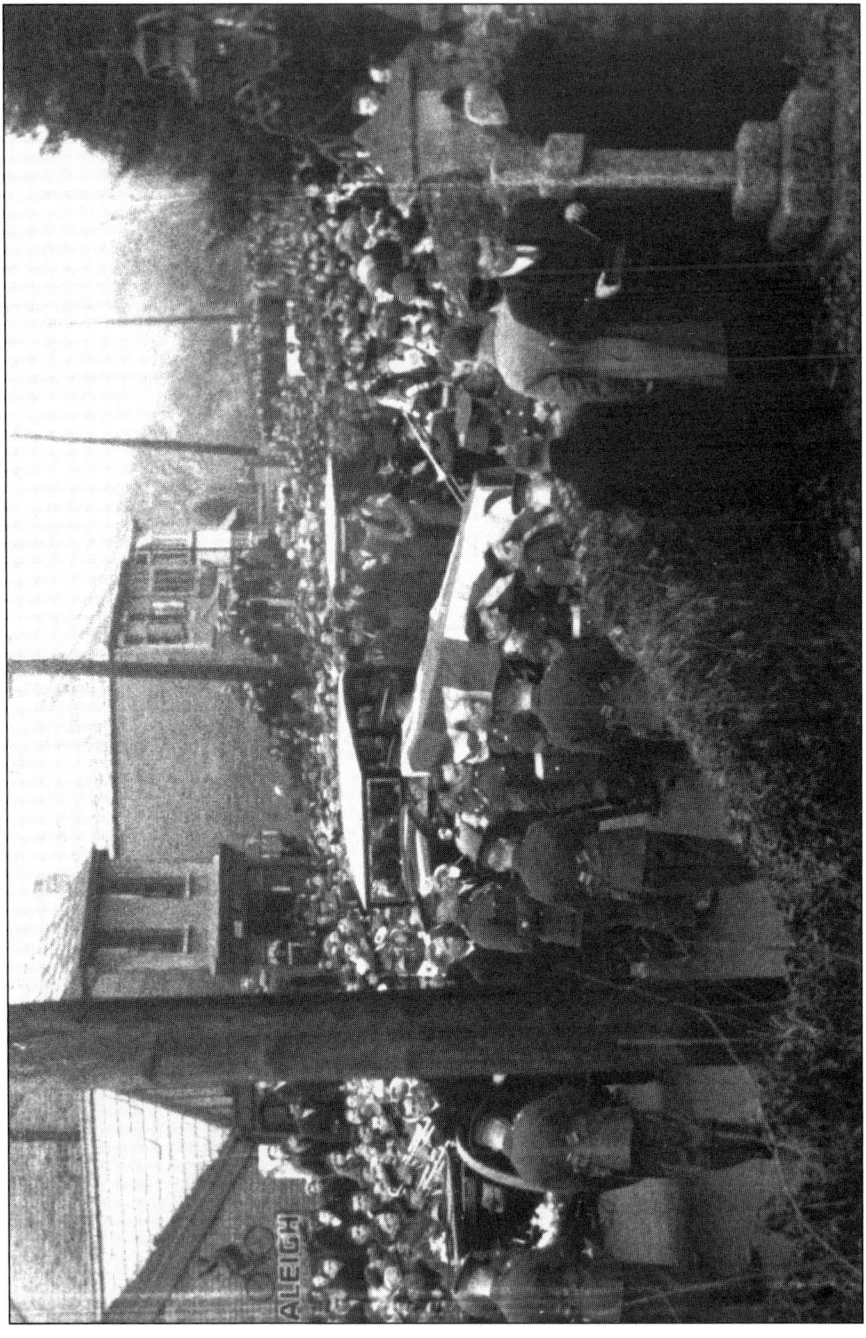
ALEIGH

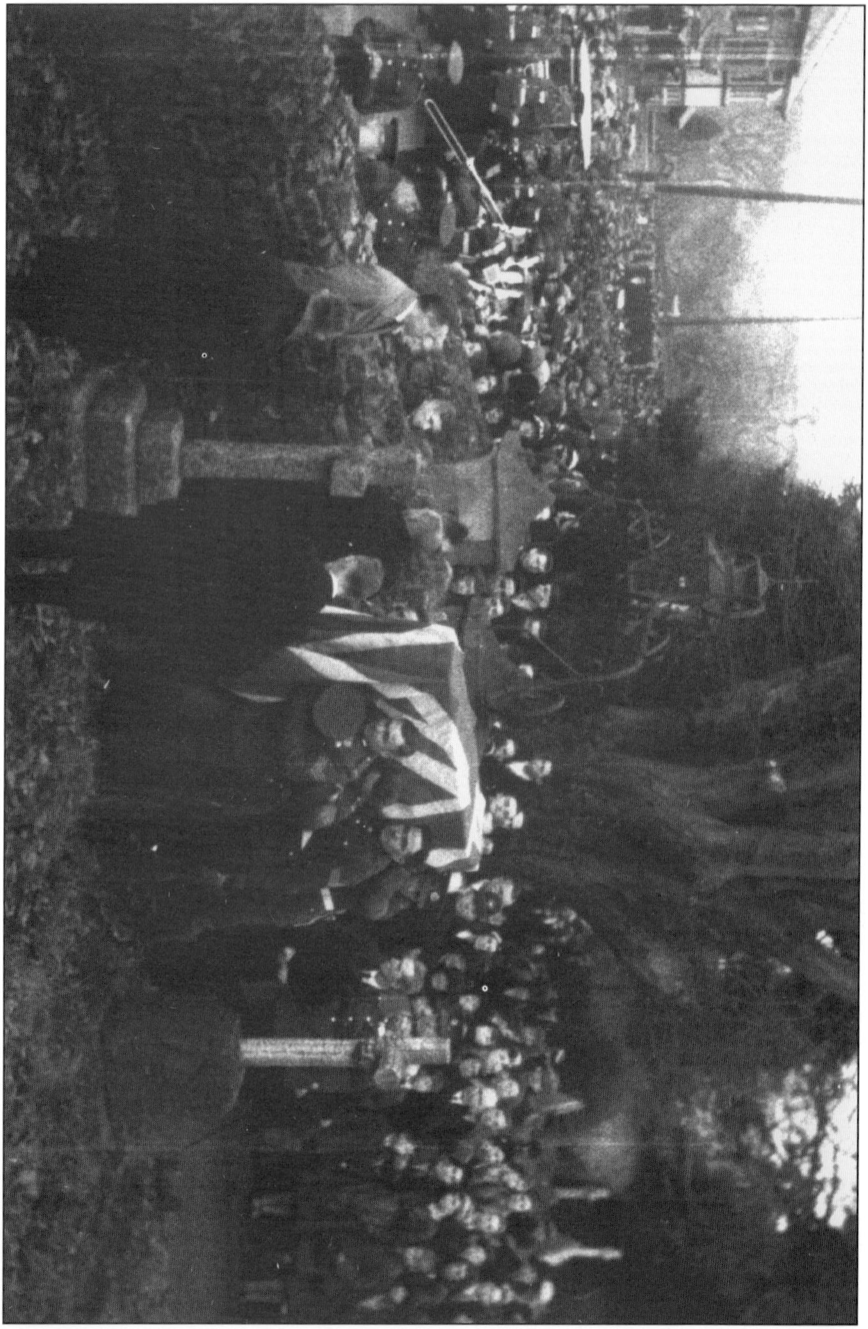

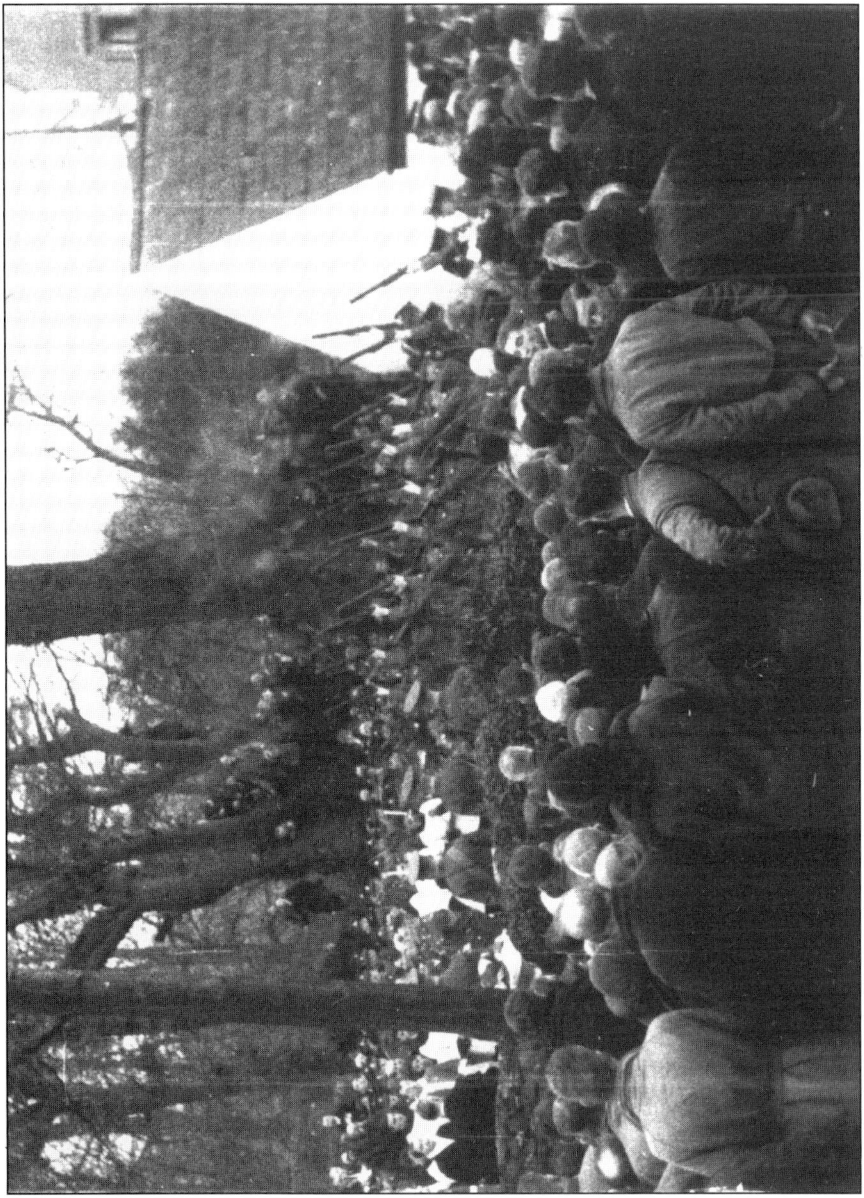

MEMORY
IN OF
JOHN FIELDING
WHO AS
PRIVATE JOHN WILLIAMS
B.COMPANY.2ND 24TH REGIMENT
WON THE
VICTORIA CROSS.
AT
THE DEFENCE OF RORKES DRIFT
DURING THE ZULU WAR.
ON
22ND/23RD JAN.1879.
DIED 25TH NOV.1932.AGED 75.
ERECTED BY
THE SOUTH WALES BORDERERS
24TH REGIMENT.
·LEST WE FORGET·

EPILOGUE

John Williams will always be remembered as a hero by the Cwmbran folk, and held in the highest esteem. Many holders of the unique award, who were to become famous for a brief time, soon settled back into obscurity and were very uncomfortable with the sudden fame thrust upon them. Also, very few benefited financially from the award. Fred Hitch V.C. went back to civilian life and became a cab driver, first with the horse-pulled variety and then the motor cab. Henry Hook V.C. did no better. After several unsuccessful jobs as a labourer, he luckily obtained a post in the British Museum, but this only amounted to dusting down the books in the General Library. Later he gained promotion and was put in charge of guarding the umbrella stand at the entrance to the reading room. Today, these brave men would in all probability be directors on some corporate management board, securing their place with the impressive letters after their names. Some, no doubt would have business managers looking after their interests, the same as the present day television personalities and pop stars. Had these social conditions existed in bygone days, John Williams would have proved very marketable, as early photographs show that he was a striking young man. It was not to be for the local hero. John Fielding lived his life in Cwmbran in a responsible manner, and when sometimes thrust unexpectantly into the limelight, he handled each occasion with a dignity that could only be inbred. When this quiet, genial, and always charming man, who did not like to hear men swearing in his presence, passed over, a great void remained in the district which would never again be filled.

After the demise of the great man, thoughts eventually turned to the future of the medal he had worn for just over fifty years. Although not as valuable in those days compared with the phenomenal sums of money paid today for a Victoria Cross, the medal obviously had tremendous sentimental value within the family. Despite still feeling the tremendous grief that one naturally feels for the loss of a close loved one, his two daughters remembered that his wish was for the Victoria Cross to go to the South Wales Borderers Museum when he died. Something in writing had been prepared to substantiate this wish, and under the supervision of Mr Fielding's old friend, Lieutenant-Colonel Gwynne Thomas, D.S.O. of Newport, the medal was donated to the recently formed South Wales Borderers Museum, Brecon. Here, thanks to his daughters and sons, the story of John Williams V.C. can still be enjoyed by many visitors up to this present day.

It is worth mentioning at this point, that the museum of the South Wales Borderers was, at this time, very much in its infancy, and existed only as an office of the commanding officer of the Brecon Depot. Here, any donated medal would be pinned to a board on the office wall, and if a request was made by a male family member to borrow a medal to be worn at some military ceremony, permission was readily given, with the agreement that the medal in question was returned within a reasonable time. This did not always serve as a satisfactory arrangement, and on the odd occasion, the staff of the depot would have to retrieve an overdue medal. Yet, it is due to the army personnel in those far off days, and right through to the present time, that the public can visit a museum unique in its own right. When one enters its profound interior, a tour, which can only be described as magical, beckons the enquiring visitor. Among the many exhibits, can be seen the bullet which lodged in the neck of Corporal John Lyons at the barricades of Rorke's Drift. When it was surgically removed over a month later, he wore the bullet, attached to a silver chain around his neck, for the remainder of his life. After his death, his widow donated the bullet and silver chain to the South Wales Borderers Museum, where it has been a great thrill for many to see this reminder of the great battle.

Time moved on in the small village of Cwmbran. A couple of years after the death of the Zulu War hero, his younger brother, Dennis Fielding, who had over 40 years military service to his credit, was honoured at Pontnewydd before leaving to become one of the famous Chelsea Pensioners. With hundreds on the waiting list for a place in the Chelsea Pensioners Home, he became the first walking resident to be admitted from Monmouthshire in forty years. He had joined the Monmouthshire Volunteers at the age of fifteen years of age, when they were commanded by Jabez Jacobs. Later he transferred to the Monmouthshire Royal Engineers, commanded by Lord Raglan, with whom he served four years before joining the famous Grenadier Guards in 1884 and continued a distinguished military career.

In 1934, a few of the remaining survivors of Rorke's Drift were among those who witnessed the laying up, in Brecon Cathedral, of the Colours carried by the old 24th Regiment during the Zulu campaign. When disaster befell the camp at Isandhlwana, Lieutenants Melvill and Coghill rode away with the Queen's Colours, but were pursued and killed by the Zulus. The Colours were found a few days later wedged in some rocks in a river.

The Eastern Valley of Monmouthshire sadly lost its last defender of Rorke's Drift at the end of September 1934. In the previous July, John Jobbins, of Machine Meadow, Pontnewynydd, had visited, as a guest, the Northern Command Tattoo in Gateshead, England. Here, with ex-Colour Sergeant Frank Bourne, D.C.M., ex-Corporal Alfred Saxty, of Newport, ex-Private Caleb Wood, and ex-Private William Cooper, all defenders of Rorke's Drift, he witnessed the re-enactment of the rearguard action. They were later presented to the crowd and received a tremendous ovation. He was not well at this time, and on returning home, his condition gradually became worse before his health eventually failed. He was interred at Trevethin Cemetery with full military honours.

With only a few of the defenders left, the story of the epic defence of Rorke's Drift was slowly being confined to the history books. It must have been a sad moment for Mrs Margaret Agg, of Abertillery, who was listening to the wireless in 1942, when an "In The Battle" item related the story of her brother Robert Jones, who helped to defend the small hospital at Rorke's Drift, and became the recipient of the Victoria Cross for his bravery.

Ex-Colour Sergeant Frank Bourne, who won the Distinguished Conduct Medal at Rorke's Drift, died in 1945, and is said to be the last of the brave defenders.

By the late nineteen forties, the large village of Cwmbran and surrounding area had a population of roughly twelve thousand people and was very much in possession of its own identity. This rapidly and amazingly changed in the nineteen fifties with the growth of the new town of Cwmbran. Within a decade, a modern town grew up, based on a garden city design. With beautiful landscaping, and splendid houses made available, the population of the area soon swelled to over fifty thousand and many of the new occupiers were from all over the British Isles. This resulted in the legend of John Williams V.C. being lost to all but the pure inhabitants of Cwmbran, mainly the old soldiers or those steeped in their regimental history.

The headstone on the grave of John Fielding had deteriorated by 1969, and was replaced by a proud and grateful regiment. Except for the inscription on this stone, surprisingly, there seemed to be no other memorial in Cwmbran which would indicate that the now large town had once accommodated a man who had taken a leading part in one of the greatest battles in British military history. This changed in 1972.

On a parcel of land known as Plas Newydd, found alongside what was then the main road from Newport to Pontypool, and opposite Saint Michael and All Angels Church, and the Greenhouse Public House, a most interesting project had been planned. At the place where many games of cricket had taken place on warm Saturday afternoons throughout the years, an imposing building was taking shape. The building, which had been started eighteen months before, was to be a much needed residential home for the physically and mentally handicapped. At a cost of £80,000, the home became the first of its kind in the county, although others were planned. The modern home was built to contain twenty five bedrooms, several of which would be fitted with hoists for those residents who were physically handicapped, and a specially adapted bathroom would also be present. At the invitation of the County Council, the local residents were invited to submit a suitable name for the project, and appropriately they suggested John Fielding House, in order to perpetuate the name of the Cwmbran hero.

Completed by the beginning of 1973, residents entered the home, but it was not until Monday June 4th, 1973 at 2.30 p.m., that the John Fielding House, at Llantarnam, Cwmbran, became ready for its official opening. By this time, the home had twenty three residents, with an age range from under eighteen years to more than fifty years. The response of the local community to their new neighbours proved highly commendable. Most of the residents worked at the county council's Glengariff training centre at Griffithstown. Several had jobs in the community, including one who worked full time at a factory, and a few others who worked in a local hostelry. The first priority since the unofficial opening had been to provide an environment in which the residents could develop, have freedom of choice, and play a useful and meaningful part within the home. This was achieved by allowing the residents to play a part in the planning of the daily routine, encouraging participation in the running of the home, in the choice of menu, and deciding what rules there should be. Mr. David Crowson, the manager of the home, did a splendid job organising the special day, and among the invited guests were fifteen relatives of the Cwmbran war hero, who had travelled from all over the country to attend. One of these was his grandson, Mr. John Fielding, of Pen-y-Mynydd, Croeserw, Cymmer. Also present were Lieutenant-Colonel C.J. Lee, Commanding, The Welsh Depot, Cwrt-y-Gollen, and members of the Welsh Regiment; Pontypool M.P. Mr Leo Abse; Alderman D.W. Evans, chairman, Monmouthshire County Council; Alderman F.I. Whatley, chairman of the social services committee; and County Councillor Doug Price, chairman of Cwmbran Council. The official opening ceremony was performed by the Rt. Hon. David Ennals, M.P., who formerly had been Minister of State for Health and Social Services in the Labour Government, and was at that present time director of "Mind" campaign, for the National Association for Mental Health. The formal speeches went well, but it was one of Mr Fielding's granddaughters, Mrs Joan Pullman, a teacher from Nuneaton, who impressed everyone by making the most interesting speech of the day which was mainly about Rorke's Drift. She had been in South Africa the previous summer, and made a point of travelling a hundred miles out of her way to visit the famous spot in Welsh military history. During her visit, she spoke to the missionary in charge of the site and explained who she was. They all seemed very pleased to see her, and when she returned home she brought a Zulu warrior's miniature shield as a memento, and which she presented to the newly opened house. The grandchildren present on that auspicious day remembered their grandfather as a loving, loveable, humble man with an immense character, who would have been hard put to understand why this new home had been named after him. With the opening ceremony completed, the family paid a simple tribute to the memory of their grandfather at his graveside. They placed a red, white and blue wreath on the grave to commemorate the opening of the home across the road.

The centenary of the battle of Rorke's Drift was celebrated extensively, and on the 18th May, 1979, a party of the Regimental Association left for South Africa. They were to take part in the Commemorations which took place at Rorke's Drift

Mr. David Ennals opens John Fielding House (Courtesy of the South Wales Argus)

John Fielding House

and Isandhlwana on 25th/26th May, of that year. Some of the descendants of those who fought in the battle accompanied the party, the cost being about £500 per head for a stay of 14 days.

In January 1980, the Cwmbran and Llantarnam Royal British Legion Club paid a tribute to John Williams V.C., by naming their newly-modernised lounge after the epic battle of Rorke's Drift. Sterling work had been carried out by the club's chairman, Mr John Blount, vice-chairman Mr E.A. Strong, club secretary, Mr J. Britton, treasurer, Mr D. Day, and all the members of the popular club to make this goal possible. It could not have been more appropriate than to have another hero of the Eastern Valley pull the first pint of beer and officially open the Rorke's Drift Lounge. This enviable task fell to Mr Edward Chapman, V.C.

And so the legend of 1395 Private John Williams has been told, and let it be retold again and again passing from one Cwmbran generation to the next. May the grand old gentleman, who lies in the corner of Saint Michael of All Angels Churchyard, rest in a well deserved peace, as the autumn leaves fall from the nearby large chestnut tree and almost cover his grave, which is but a few yards from the busy road carrying hundreds of unsuspecting motorists each day. Young recruits passing through the Welsh Depot continue to hear of the brave deeds of the Cwmbran man, but, for Private John Williams, who had many years before experienced one shining moment in time, the smoke, rolling valleys, and surging impis of Rorke's Drift, are no more.

REFERENCES

1. Slater's Directory 1862.

2. Webster & Co. Commercial Directory 1865.

3. Paton, George; Glennie, Farquhar; Penn Symons, William (editors), *Historical Records of the 24th Regiment, from its formation, in 1689* (London: Simpkin, Marshall, Hamilton, Kent & Co., 1892), pp. 208-09.

4. *Free Press of Monmouthshire,* January 27th, 1927.

5. *Western Mail & South Wales News,* January 22nd, 1929.

6. *Free Press of Monmouthshire,* April 1st, 1932.

7. Atkinson C.T., *The South Wales Borderers, 24th Foot, 1689-1937.* p. 326.

8. Norris-Newman, Charles L., *In Zululand with the British throughout the War of 1879* (London: W.H. Allen & Co., 1880), p.16.

9. *The Dover Express,* April 25th, 1879.

10. *The Pontypool Free Press,* March 1st, 1879.

11. *The Pontypool Free Press,* March 8th, 1879.

12. *The Pontypool Free Press,* March 8th, 1879.

13. *Star of Gwent,* March 6th, 1879,

14. *South Wales Daily Telegraph,* March 29th, 1879.

15. *The Pontypool Free Press,* March 29th, 1879.

16. *The South Wales Daily Telegraph,* March 24th, 1879.

17. *The Pontypool Free Press,* March 29, 1879.

18. *The Pontypool Free Press*, April 5th, 1879.

19. *The Pontypool Free Press*, April 12th, 1879.

20. *The South Wales Daily Telegraph,* March 27th, 1879.

21. *The Pontypool Free Press*, April 19th, 1879.

22. *Free Press of Monmouthshire,* February 27th, 1931.

23. *The Natal Colonist*, January 15th, 1880, p.3.

24. Mrs Kathleen Couzens, Cwmbran, (granddaughter of John Fielding) owner of one of the original scrolls; *The Natal Colonist,* January 15th, 1880.

25. *South Wales Argus*, January 1980.

26. The South Wales Borderers and Monmouthshire Regimental Museum of The Royal Regiment of Wales.

27. *The Graphic,* April 10th, 1880, p.366.

28. *The Graphic*, April 10th, 1880, p.372.

29. The South Wales Borderers and Monmouthshire Regimental Museum of The Royal Regiment of Wales.

30. Atkinson, C.T., *The South Wales Borderers, 24th Foot, 1689-1937.* pp. 367-368.

31. Atkinson, C.T., *The South Wales Borderers, 24th Foot, 1689-1937.* p. 362.

32. *Pontypool Free Press,* September 6th and 20th, 1879; December 12th, 1879.

33. *The Times*, June 28th, 1920.

34. *The Free Press of Monmouthshire*, June 11th, 1926.

35. *The Times*, November 9th, 11th, and 12th, 1929.

36. *The Free Press of Monmouthshire,* November 15th, 1929.

37. *The Times,* November 26th, 1932; *Western Mail*, November 30th, 1932; *Free Press of Monmouthshire*, December 2nd, 1932; *South Wales Argus,* November 30th, 1932.

APPENDIX

The Monmouthshire Beacon, March 29th, 1879.

Rorke's Drift, Natal, South Africa.
February 6th, 1879.

Dear Father and Mother,-I now have the pleasure to send you a few lines, hoping they will find you quite well, as they leave me at present. Since I wrote to you last we have had a deal of hard work and terrible fighting. But before you receive this letter I expect you have heard something about it from the newspapers; but I will tell you a little about what I have seen myself.

On the 22nd of January, about 4.0 a.m., the General left camp with about half the Division in search of the Kaffirs; they threw out a few thousand men as a decoy for our troops to follow, which they did instead of following the main body of the Kaffir Army. When our men got about 16 miles out of camp they could see large numbers of the enemy approaching the camp which they had just left.

But our wise Commanders did not think it necessary to turn back and protect the camp until it was too late; they kept on marching after the other few men in the front. Well, there were about 20,000 Zulus attacking the camp (but mind, I was about 12 miles away with our Company, in charge of the commissary stores). There was left in the camp five companies of the 1-24th (1st Company G) of our picquet, and a lot more of our men on guard, and on the staff, officers' servants and cooks, five little band-boys, and our new bandmaster just come to our Regiment, and there were a lot of volunteers left in camp, and two guns of the Royal Artillery. The guns opened fire on them, but it was no use; as fast as the fire mowed them down, their place was filled up again by more of them. All our men that fell, and especially the little boys, were cut to pieces by the Zulus. They are not satisfied with killing us, but they mutilate the body afterwards.

These names I mention are known very well by me and you, - poor Alf Farr, Charlie Long, George Morris, Harry Smith (who used to live on Sowhill), Dick Treverton and Will Rees. These have been killed. There were about 16 white men that escaped from the camp out of about 900 men. All the others, officers and men, were killed.

There were two officers who escaped on horseback with the colours of the 1-24th; they got down to a river called the Buffalo, when they were both knocked over, and the colours were found a few days after by the side of the two poor officers. All who did escape were on horseback.

At night the General received a message from the camp to say it was taken, and all the ammunition, two guns, about 1,000 rifles and thousands of pounds in cash. "Well," the General says this to the men, "we must take the camp with the point of a bayonet"; and they first had to shell the camp with the six guns the General had out with him. When the men got back to camp they could see the Zulus retiring, and the men had to sleep that night amongst the dead, and some terrible sights there were; but there were say about ten blacks killed to each white man.

Before it was daylight in the morning, what was left of our poor soldiers had to retire upon the stores where I was with about 120 men of our Company and Volunteers. The day before, four men on horseback, who had escaped from the camp, arrived at the stores and told us what had happened. This was about 3 o'clock in the afternoon of the 22nd January. We at once let our tents fall to the ground, and got inside the stores and made a small fort with sacks of grain. Just as we finished our little fort we could see thousands of niggers coming down on our little body of men. At the end of the fort was a large house which had been used as a hospital, the owners of which were Swedes, who fled as soon as the Zulus were in sight. There was a lot of sick men in the hospital at the time; one poor Sergeant (Maxfield) was insane, and he was burned alive, or killed and then burnt. Well, we fought hard from about 3.30 p.m. till the following morning, when they retired; they had killed about 12 of our men, but we killed at least 450 of them. They were charging over the sacks but we repulsed them. All that night a minister in the fort was praying that they would go away. God help us and give us the victory. In the morning we could see in the distance a large body of men. We did not at first recognise them, but after a bit we could see the welcome redcoats retiring on us from the other unfortunate camp. We then gave a hearty cheer, as we felt safe when we were all together. Nothing important has happened since the 22nd; but we have ever since been making our fort stronger, and we sleep in our clothes every night on the look-out. One of the poor fellows who was wounded is a Corporal Lyons (he used to go about with Jim Sullivan), but he is expected to get over it. Poor M. Morgan is here very bad with fever, but he seems to be getting over it. The General has sent to England for 10,000 more troops. We shall advance no further till they come out here. I send my kind love to my brothers and sisters, to Mrs Sullivan and all friends, thanking God I am well, and hoping you are all the same.

Your affectionate son,
J. Jobbins.

When you write address:-No 1,061, J Jobbins, B. Company 2-24th Reg., Natal, South Africa. Goodbye and bless you all.

The Cambrian, June 13th, 1879.
Pontypool Free Press, June 14th, 1879.

Statement by 1112 Corporal John Lyons, 2/24th Regiment.

I belong to B Company of the 2/24th, under Lieutenant Bromhead. I went up to Greytown with Private Hitch, who was one of the same company. We arrived at Rorke's Drift about 5th January. I saw Private Evans of the Mounted Infantry, riding up at full gallop, without either coat or cap on, and I, of course, thought there was something up.

Hitch had by this time reported that the Zulus were in sight, and we were scarcely finished before they were upon us. We were told not to fire without orders. This, I suppose was to make sure that the advancing force was really Zulu. Only a few seconds elapsed before the full character of it was made known to us. The Zulus did not shout, as they generally do; but, after extending and forming a half-moon, they steadily advanced and kept up a tremendous fire. I took up a position to check the fire from the enemy's right flank, as it was thought the crack shots would go up there. Corporal Allen and several men with me, and we all consider we did good service. Lieutenant Bromhead was on the right face, firing over the mealies with a Martini-Henry. Mr Chard was also very busy. I only turned round once to see this, and in this brief interval I saw Private Cole shot, and he fell dead. Seeing this, I kept myself more over the bags, knowing that the shot which had hit him had come over our heads, and I was determined to check this flank firing as much as possible. I become thus more exposed, and so did Corporal Allen. We fired many shots, and I said to my comrade, 'They (the Zulus) are falling fast over there,' and he replied 'Yes, we are giving it to them.' I saw many Zulus killed on the hill.

About half past seven, as near as I can tell, after we had been fighting two or three hours, I received a shot through the right side of the neck. The ball lodged in the back, striking the spine, and was not extracted till five weeks afterwards. My right arm was partially disabled. I said, 'Give it to them, Allen. I am done; I am dying,' and he replied, 'All right Jack'; and while I was speaking to him I saw a hole in the right sleeve of his jacket, and I said, 'Allen, you are shot,' and he replied, 'Yes, goodbye.' He walked away, with blood running from his arm, and he helped to serve out ammunition all night. All I could do as I lay on the ground was to encourage the men, and I did so as long as I was able to open my mouth. Every man fought dearly for his life, but we were all determined to sell our lives like soldiers, and to keep up the credit of our regiment. Mr. Dalton, who has since received a commission, deserves any amount of praise.

Free Press of Monmouthshire April 18th, 1913.

RORKE'S DRIFT

Sir, - After hearing different statements concerning the battle of Rorke's Drift, which I think should be corrected, I beg a short space in your paper to do so, in the interest of Justice to those left alive after their heroic defence. I, Gunner A. Evans, "N" Battery, 5th Brigade R.A., of which battery half was lost at Isandhlwana, when the terrible disaster occurred to that notable regiment, the 24th Warwickshire's, now the South Wales Borderers, feel it my duty, being one of the number, to correct the statements I read time after time in the papers.

First of all let me say that anyone who would like to criticise this statement is at liberty to do so while I live, so that I may answer any questions they would like to ask me. I beg to state that after the disaster of Isandhlwana I saw the scout from Isandhlwana gallop to Rorke's Drift to warn them that the Zulus were advancing on that place. This scout was minus any arms or clothing but Jersey and pants, and knowing the danger we were in, made all haste to come to us.

This message was first given to Dr. Reynolds, between 2 and 2.30 in the afternoon. Then he at once set the men to work to form a laager from the hospital to the shore. Meanwhile Lieut.s Bromhead and Chard were giving orders elsewhere and making preparations for the best resistance possible with so small a number of men, and many of them sick. I may say that under adverse circumstances as these were, this laager and defences was built from 4 to 4.30pm. I was then standing in the doorway of the hospital, and witnessed five Zulus come in front of the doorway, jumping in their mad frenzy, flushed with their late victory.

Just at this moment my newest mates were Adams and Jenkins, of the 24th Regt. What became of these men I can't say, I never saw them after. There were in all 30 casualties, 17 killed, and 13 wounded, out of the 96 men. The number of rifles in action was 85, and every man a man, and when you know that 17,000 rounds of ammunition were fired during the action, I think you will agree with me that all men were heroes of the first water. Yet there is a lot said now that is not true. There were killed at this battle 700 of the bravest tribe in South Africa, within six hundred yards of the hospital, therefore the ammunition was well spent.

No doubt many wonder what I, a R.A. man, was doing at Rorke's Drift. I was left there sick, but not too sick but that I could not help my comrades in arms to defend our position, and could say many things about it. I beg to inform the Editor of the "Daily Sketch," who published the account of the funeral of V.C. Hitch, that Major H.J. Williams is not a survivor of Rorke's Drift. There was no officer of that name at all. There are several men left alive today, myself included, in the immediate neighbourhood in which I live, one of them a V.C. man. On the 23rd January I witnessed the burial of those men who were killed on the 22nd, in this historic battle, in two large holes, which our native pioneers had dug for that purpose, and which was done on the return of the Column under General Chelmsford from Isandhlwana.

My position at this time was on the parapet, alongside Lt. Chard, and watching them, the Column, coming down to the pontoon which Dr Reynolds and other officers, Lieut.s Bromhead and Chard, thought were Zulus dressed in our men's clothing, and they asked me to mount the sack and look through the field glasses. As soon as I got there I told them I did not want the glasses for I could see it was our men, and I could see a division of grey horses in the middle of the Infantry. I took up my former position alongside Lt. Chard, on the parapet, until Lord Chelmsford came and spoke to Lt. Chard, thanking him for the way we held the position during the night. Shortly after this our brave men followed up to the laager and into the bush, where they found heaps of dead bodies, and I shall never forget the sound of the click as they fixed bayonets, and there took some revenge for Isandhlwana.

Mr Editor, this statement is made by one who was presented to her late Majesty - Queen Victoria - with three others, making two from Rorke's Drift, and two who escaped from Isandhlwana. This was in July, 1882.

(Signed)
A. Evans,

Spring Gardens, Varteg, Mon.

Western Mail May 20th, 1914.

Another Soldier Hero
Third Rorke's Drift Survivor
In South Wales

Honoured By Queen Victoria

As well as Mr John Jones, the Merthyr veteran, and Private John Williams, V.C., of Cwmbran, whose reminiscences were published in the Western Mail recently, there is living in South Wales another of the heroes whose wonderful defence of Rorke's Drift astonished the Empire. He is ex-Gunner Evans, Spring Gardens, Varteg, Pontypool.

It was in 1874 that the ex-gunner joined the Army, for in that year he enlisted in the Royal Field Artillery at Newport. His first campaign was in the Kaffir War of 1877, and it involved long marches and much bush fighting. Then came the Zulu War. His battery marched with the field column to Isandhlwana, leaving him in hospital at Rorke's Drift. One day while he was there a survivor from Isandhlwana, a Natal Carbineer, came there at full gallop to tell them of the disaster, and to warn them that the Zulu were moving on the drift. Immediately preparations began, and under the direction of Lieutenant Bromhead and Dr. Reynolds, Army Surgeon, a laager was formed. Ex-Gunner Evans helped in its formation and in the removal of the helpless invalids from the hospital, and later in the twelve hour defence, which ended in the repulse of the enemy.

Apart from Rorke's Drift, ex-Gunner Evans has many tales to tell. He was one of the firing party at the burial of the Prince Imperial. No volleys were fired - ammunition was scarce, and all that was done was to snap the triggers. Afterwards the ex-gunner served in the first Boer War, and in the defence of Potchefstroom, which was besieged by the Boers, he was wounded in the back by a bullet which came through an embrasure into the gun-pit. Evans suffered from enteric fever during an epidemic which caused many deaths, including that of Captain Justice, of Newport. The succession of deaths led to the pipers of the Scots Fusiliers to march around the camp on many evenings at tattoo, playing laments.

On return to England the battery was ordered to Winsor Park for inspection by the late Queen Victoria. As a veteran of three campaigns, and as a defender of Rorke's Drift, Evans was especially brought under the notice of Queen Victoria, who spoke a few words to each. About this time one of the officers of the battery was Captain Rundle, now Governor of Malta. Evans was on the point of being discharged from the Army when the first Egyptian War broke out. At once he applied to have his discharge cancelled, and volunteered for the front. He served at Tel-el Kebir, and remembers having to drink water from canals in which floated the dead bodies of men and animals. Within a short time cholera broke out in the camp.

Evans possesses the South African medal with dates 1877-78-79 - the full significance of which only soldiers can understand - the Egyptian medal, and the Khedive's Star.

Some years ago much was done for the Crimean veterans. Surely the time has come to do something for the survivors of later campaigns. The Welsh survivors of Rorke's Drift have a strong claim on the Principality. Another claim is for a bar for Rorke's Drift. Pressure by the Welsh members of Parliament on the Secretary of War could right this neglect.

Free Press of Monmouthshire January 21st, 1927.

Rorke's Drift Hero
Mr William Osborne
Blaenavon

Description of Fight

Yet another Rorke's Drift hero has been "discovered", and on this occasion at Blaenavon, in the person of William Osborne, who resides with his wife at 79, Cambrian Row. Mr Osborne, who will be 69 on Feb. 20th, saw active service in the Kaffir War of '77, and the Zulu Wars of '78 and '79, in the old 24th Foot (South Wales Borderers).

Born at Duke's Street, Blaenavon, Mr William Osborne (the son of Mr Thomas Osborne, who was employed at the Blaenavon Co.'s Mills), when quite a youngster, joined the Regular Army, and took the Queens silver coin at Pontypool. He was at once transfered to Brecon and shortly afterwards moved to Chatham. In November of the same year he was put on draft for Africa, and sailed from Portsmouth in the old Himalaya. Mr Osborne distinctly remembers that one of the first jobs when going on board was to empty the ticks of old straw, which was then taken to the quarter master for refilling. The voyage, which lasted about five weeks, was a good one, no heavy weather encountered. Upon landing, the troops entrained and travelled via Durban to King William's Town. From here a march lasting between two and three weeks brought them in touch with the enemy.

The incident at Rorke's Drift is graphically described by Mr Osborne. A fatigue party of about 100 were to hold off for the commissariat duties and preparing food for the main column. The small company was in the charge of a captain and no untoward incident happened for some time. The "kitchen" was an outdoor one, adjacent to a house which had been occupied by a Dutchman who carried on the business of a shoemaker. This house, with a thatched roof, had been vacated when the British reached it, the only living things left being a domestic cat and an old sow. Sixteen hoggets (or small pigs) had been drowned, evidently by the savages, who were afraid of the swine. "But we saved the old pig," said Mr Osborne, "and had some fine meat from her."

An interesting description of the method of baking the bread was given. Large ant-hills, were dotted around the place. At the top of each of these a hole would be made, and, at the bottom, a cavity, into which a fire would be placed, and soon the ants would emerge in millions from the hole at the top. The fire would then be taken out and leavened dough would be placed in the cavity, which would quickly bake. (This is a principle employed even today, and is known as the "Aldershot oven,")

The first intermation that the enemy were approaching the camp was given by one of the company, who had been washing at the river, and it was discovered that the camp, or dump, had been cut off from the main column. Preparations were rapidly made for defending Rorke' House, which besides being used for a store for food, was also a hospital. Including the "casualties" there were in all about 100 men. The Zulus numbered between 3,000 and 4,000 and practically naked, attacked the drift with great courage in face of deadly rifle fire. Their weapons were mostly assegais (spears), but that they were in possession of some ammunition is proved by the fact that Corporal Jack Lines (at one time a postman in the Eastern Valley) received a bullet wound in the back of the neck, "which bullet his wife still possesses," said Mr Osborne.

"We had seventeen hours of hard fighting," continued the narrator of the story. "If we were all third-class shots it would have been all over for us. They came in their thousands, and we made them jump! We took six or seven prisoners, but we sent them out in the open again. If you didn't catch 'em smart as they put their hands up, they were gone like a dart! Jack Lines (Lyons) and I were firing together with our ammunition placed on the wall besides us. The corporal was in the act of raising his rifle when his arms dropped helplessly to his sides from a bullet wound in the back of the neck. The enemy set the thatched roof afire, but we pulled the roof off during the night to stop that little game. It was 17 hours before the relief came.

Mr Osborne remembers a few of those who were in the engagement, including Captain Browning and Jack Williams, V.C. (Cwmbran)

From Africa Mr Osborne was sent to Gibraltar, and from there to India, where he completed his six years regular service. He returned to Blaenavon in 1883 at 26 years of age, and began work underground for the Blaenavon Co. After his return he married Miss Martha Whitcombe, of Abersychan. There was one daughter (Mrs S. Williams) and an adopted son, Mr Wm. Osborne (Wm. Burnell), the latter who figures in Blaenavon billiard circles.

Africa A Great Country

Asked for his opinion of the countries he had visited, Mr Osborne sang the praises of Africa, which he thought, was the greatest country in the world. There are two things which he treasures. One is his medal with three bars which Mrs Osborne wears as a brooch, and the other is a Bible, presented by the ladies of the Rorke's Drift Testimonial Fund, and signed by "Miss Wilkinson."

Gunner Abraham Evans, Died May 4th, 1915
Spring Gardens, Varteg, Pontypool.

South Wales Argus, June 3rd, 1914.

AT RORKE'S DRIFT.

Newport Veteran's Story.
A Rescue from Burning Hospital.

Survivors of the small company who gallantly held Rorke's Drift against an overwhelming force of victory-flushed Zulus are few in number, but the discovery of one apparently leads to the discovery of others. Private John Williams, V.C., of Cwmbran, was no sooner thrust into the limelight than Private Sam Pitt, of Nantymoel, was unearthed, and now it is learned that there is living in Newport another member of the brave band which added such lustre to British arms.

Mr. John Murphy, of 41, Witham Street, Newport, belonged to the old 24th Regiment, and after going through the Kaffir War played his part in the Zulu campaign. He tells a very similar story to that narrated by Private Sam Pitt, and January, 1879, he declares, has never been, and is not likely ever to be, effaced from his memory.

HANDFUL AGAINST THOUSANDS.

It was on January 22nd that the messenger from Isandhulu reached them with the direful tidings that the British advance force had been almost wiped out. They knew then what to expect, but, handful as they were, there were no cowards among them, and they were determined either to thrash the Zulus or die fighting to the last. Indeed, he says, there was no other thing to do, for Cetewayo's warriors had few notions in the way of dealing mercifully with a foe they had the power to slaughter.

To fix up defences worthy of the name did not appear to be a very hopeful task, for they had no fortifications, simply two old mission rooms, one of which was used as a hospital and the other for the storage of provisions, ammunition, etc. Apart from invalids, the British force numbered 84, and it was realised that their visitors would make them look a little lot indeed. Bags of biscuits and mealies formed a hastily-improvised entrenchment, and this was all that was between them and the advancing horde.

Early in the afternoon the enemy were sighted, and soon the country around was black with them. In another hour they were within rifle range, and the ghastly fun began. The fire, however, seemed to make no difference, and on they rolled, the defenders having eventually to retire to an inner "fortification." It was a terrible struggle, but nothing to the fight at close quarters as darkness set in. Private Murphy described the fight at length, but as this is a matter of history-familiar, it is to be hoped, to all-the details need not be given further.

RESCUE FROM HOSPITAL.

One incident, however, should be narrated. When the hospital caught fire, and it was necessary to get the inmates out, Private Murphy did his full share of the work, and one difficult task which fell to his lot was pulling through the window a private named Connolly, who had a broken leg. The next man near that particular spot was shot through the head.

Meanwhile the battle continued to rage, but eventually the fine defence prevailed, and the enemy drew off. The British casualties were few, the Zulus had lost hundreds-for in the morning the ground was covered with their dead and dying.

Private Murphy was very emphatic on one point, and, though he may be in error, it is perhaps worth recording that he thinks the part played by certain officers was unduly extolled at the time and since. They were not, he declares, nearly so conspicuous in the fight as they have been made out to be.

Murphy (who at Rorke's Drift was slightly wounded in the foot) was 24 years in the Army, and then, having reached the age of 60, had to leave, but declares that at the time he felt fit to serve another 24.

Western Mail, January 22nd, 1929.

STORY OF RORKE'S DRIFT.

Stirring Tale of Pte.
J. Williams, V.C.

"I was born at Abergavenny in 1858," he said, "and 'listed on January 22, 1877- two years to the day before the fight at Rorke's Drift. We got to South Africa in the beginning of 1878, and after remaining at Bailey's Post some time were sent up country. While there, by the way, Capt. A.G. Godwin-Austen (whose brother was killed at Isandhlwana), was our captain, and Lieut. Bromhead was our lieutenant. We had a brush with the Kaffirs, and Capt. Austen was wounded and went home. He was shot in the loins by a Hottentot who was up a tree. We very soon settled accounts with him. We had him out of that tree like one o'clock. Well, we moved up to Pietermaritzburg, and thence to Rorke's Drift.

"This, of course, was a mission station, and consisted of a few low buildings. The first lot of the regiment crossed on January 11th to the Bashi Valley and soon had an encounter with the Zulus, and then they moved on to Isandhlwana, and you know what happened there. My company was left at Rorke's Drift in charge of the hospital there, as well as the commissariat.

95 AGAINST 3,000.

"We first heard of the great disaster from Col. Groom, who told us about Lieuts. Melvill and Coghill. We had it, too, from the chaplain, the Rev. W. Smith. He is still living, I believe, but in any case I would like to say what a fine man he was, a true hero, who during the night that followed rendered magnificent service.

"I can see it all now as clearly as I saw it on that day. There were 95 of us at that post, and we knew that 3,000 Zulus, flushed with victory and mad for more slaughter, would soon be upon us. We had just time. It was 3.30 in the afternoon when we saw them begin to round the hill, and never did an enemy seem to have an easier prey. We had no more time to improvise barricades with biscuit tins and mealie bags, and now they were upon us.

"What did I feel? I don't know that I felt anymore than all the others felt. In his ordinary life a man often contemplates some possibility and feels he would be unable to face it, but when it happens he does face it. He finds himself up against it, and goes through with it. That is just about what happened to all of us.

"We knew the seriousness of the affair, but we had no time to sit down and think about it. And now there were the Zulus, and there was one watchword for all of us - we must keep the enemy at bay. I heard that many times during the night that followed.

NO TIME TO THINK

"Beside, when the enemy appeared we had precious little time for thinking. The attack started at 3.30 in the afternoon, and for the next eighteen hours we knew all about it."

Here Pte. John Williams began to show less inclination to talk. One, naturally, wanted him to describe that night of hell and how he helped to save the wounded and the sick. But he would say little more than it was recorded in the official "Gazette." Therein it is told that -

"Pte. John Williams was posted with Pte. Joseph Williams and Pte. William Horrigan in a distant room of the hospital, which they held for more than an hour, so long as they had a round of ammunition left. As communication was for a time cut off, the Zulus were able to advance and burst open the door. They dragged out Pte. Joseph Williams and two of the patients, and assegaid them. Whilst the Zulus were occupied with the slaughter of these men a lull took place, during which Pte. John Williams with two patients, who were the only men now left alive in this ward, succeeded in knocking a hole in the partition and taking the two patients into the next ward, where he found Pte. Hook. These two men together, one working whilst the other fought and held the enemy at bay with his bayonet, broke through three more partitions, and were thus enabled to bring eight patients through a small window into the rear line of defence."

"Yes," proceeded Pte. John Williams, "it was a terrible time. All we were concerned with was to keep the enemy at bay and to save the patients if we could. While they were killing poor Joe Williams and Horrigan I was as busy as I could be knocking that hole in the partition."

All he would add was that when his share in the fighting was ended he had just two rounds of ammunition left.